CW00516256

THE COMPLETE UK AIR FRYER COOKBOOK

100 Delicious, Easy & Healthy Recipes
To Improve Your Diet &
Make Cooking Fun & Effortless
With British Ingredients & Measurements

By

Fearne Prentice

A BOOK FROM THE
COOKING WITH FEARNE
SERIES

A BOOK FROM THE
COOKING WITH FEARNE
SERIES

The Air Fryer will change the way we cook and eat forever!

This book consists of 7 different sections, each complete with comprehensive recipes and a list of required ingredients. You'll never need another Air Fryer cookbook again!

Thank you for buying this book by Fearne Prentice today, and don't forget to stay tuned for more recipes under the "Cooking with Fearne" series!

DON'T FORGET THAT THIS PURCHASE COMES WITH A FREE BOOK!

How To Access Your BONUS Coloured Photos & Beautifully Designed Bonus Book For the Top Recipes:

To keep printing costs down, we sadly couldn't include coloured pictures inside this print book, otherwise we would've had to charge at least triple the price if not more.

So, to make sure you still have access to coloured photos, we have created a PDF version of the top recipes from this book with supplementary images, completely free for you.

Just follow the steps below to access it via the QR Code (found inside the book upon purchase), or click the link if you are reading this on your Phone / Device.

1. *Unlock your phone & open up the phone's camera*

2. *Make sure you are using the "back" camera (as if you were taking a photo of someone) and point it towards the QR code at the bottom of the page.*

3. *Tap your phone's screen exactly where the QR code is.*

4. *A link / pop up will appear. Simply tap that (and make sure you have internet connection) and the FREE PDF containing the coloured images should appear.*

5. *You now have access to this whenever you want, simply bookmark it or download it and you can take it wherever you want!*

We hope this makes up for not being able to print with coloured photos and that you love the recipes! Thank you!

TABLE OF CONTENTS

1 | INTRODUCTION

AUTHOR'S NOTE

Fried foods! From fish and chips to chicken nuggets, cheese sticks, and doughnuts, these popular meals are oh-so-delicious! But – and there is a big "but" – eating a lot of fried foods can have harmful effects on your health! As a popular cooking method, frying adds so many calories and trans-fats to your foods. What's worse, fried foods are typically dipped in flour, eggs, and breadcrumbs that absorb fat and drastically increase the calorie content of your meals. If we are not eating right, we typically have cravings, especially for fatty foods. We experience frequent hunger as well as problems with excess weight, and inconsistent and low-energy levels during the day. Luckily, making the right food choices and finding a healthy cooking method can help you eat better and feel better!

I love experimenting with cool kitchen gadgets almost as much as I love food and cooking. Thus, I stumbled upon a commercial for an air fryer and I thought, "It sounds interesting. Let's explore this!" Shortly after that, I bought my first air fryer, and it was love at first sight! I couldn't wait to cook with this new-fangled kitchen companion!

After testing a wide range of recipes in my air fryer, I think I finally cracked the code! Like most of us, I started with fish and chips, pigs in blankets, and roasted veggies. Then I decided to cook my family favourites, such as casseroles, French toast, sandwiches, and cakes in my air fryer. Adapting old-fashioned recipes from the oven and skillet to the air fryer was an amazing adventure! I rounded off my journey by making brownies, cookies, and even mince pies in my air fryer.

In keeping with the latest health trends, I also wanted to explore nutritional facts about air-fried foods. Therefore, my recipes also contain nutritional analysis. I created recipes that anyone can use, even beginners. That's how this collection was created!

As we mentioned, fried foods are not intended to be staples of a well-balanced diet; they contain significant amounts of fats and calories. Deep-fried, commercial foods are not a good choice, but air-fried food is another story. What are the basic postulates of a healthy diet, according to nutrition experts? First and foremost, aim to eat five servings of fruit and vegetables per day; further, avoid trans fats. And last but not least, foods should be boiled, steamed, baked, and occasionally grilled. Although health experts recommend eating a variety of healthy, fresh, and minimally-processed foods, abstaining from junk foods and takeout remains the most difficult change we should make to lose weight and live healthier.

For many dieters, baked or boiled foods are not satisfying. Dieters often complain about lack of flavour as well as lack of time for cooking at home. My air Fryer changed the way I cook forever! It helped me to take my culinary skills to the next level. I also lost weight along the way. I became much healthier and happier with my weight! High-powered kitchen tools are often required for producing the best results with your favourite foods. When it comes to your heath, good-quality equipment is a top priority. Good kitchen tools will save you a great deal of time, making cooking a pleasure rather than a hassle. It will also save you money and frustration.

Studies have proven that air frying is one of the healthiest methods of preparing food! These studies have shown a significantly lower amount of harmful chemicals in fried foods (up to 90%). Your foods retain most of their natural nutrients that are oftentimes lost during deep-frying and long cooking. Air frying is a simple way to enjoy your favourite veggies, bringing out their natural flavours and colours; even dull vegetables such as beetroot, courgetti, and broccoli will taste and look better with the power of air frying. Unlike conventional cooking methods, air frying is a gentler cooking method, so it is almost impossible to overcook meals. Finally, an air fryer will make cleaning a cinch!

The primary goals of this cookbook are to break bad eating habits and to provide good alternatives to junk food, cooking your favourites (such as fish and chips, burgers, and cakes) in a new, healthier way. These recipes will help you turn your favourite cheat foods into a good, pleasurable addition to a well-balanced diet. We will use simple, seasonal, and wholesome ingredients and avoid highly-refined ingredients as much as possible. Hopefully, with your air fryer, there will be no more excuses for bad eating habits. Plus, your cravings for fried foods will be satisfied. You'll be amazed by the flavours of air-fried foods! Remember, cooking is an art, and there is always room for improvement and new discoveries. Your cooking skills will continue to evolve as you continue to learn more about air frying. Since every journey begins with the first step, let's get going!

EVERYTHING YOU NEED TO KNOW ABOUT AIR FRYERS

An air fryer typically consists of electric heating elements, a cooking chamber, a drawer (or holder with a handle), a high-speed fan, air vents, and a control panel (or the power indicator and the temperature indicator). Further, most air fryers are equipped with digital displays, so you can easily set the cooking time and temperature. Thanks to these features, you do not have to worry about overcooking or undercooking your food. While the food is in the cooking basket, hot air goes up to 200 degrees C, using rapid air technology to circulate around your food. There is a fan that is designed to distribute the hot air evenly throughout the cooking chamber. Ultimately, there is a special drawer with a removable cooking basket, which is coated with a non-stick material. Make sure to put your food only into the cooking basket.

When it comes to other equipment for your new kitchen appliance, you can use non-stick, perforated baking trays, cupcake cases, loaf tins, waffle moulds, tartlet moulds, silicone tongs and brushes, wooden spatulas, and paper oven liners. Doubtlessly, having essential kitchen equipment and utensils will help you follow the recipes effortlessly and efficiently. They include paper and tea towels, knives, prep bowls, measuring tools, peeler, wire whisk, food processor, and cutting board.

How does it work in practice? The whole cooking process is easy and fun to follow. Place the ingredients in the lightly greased cooking basket, set the time and temperature, and then wait for your meal to cook! It's so easy! To illustrate, let's say you want to prepare fish and chips for lunch. You can soak them in a hot cooking oil, using a regular pan. However, you can cook your meal with a few drizzles of healthy oil and get an even better taste and that familiar, crunchy texture. A greasy mess and excess calories become a matter of the past with your air fryer! In short, just place all the ingredients in the cooking basket, and then pop the whole thing in your machine. You can enjoy crunchy bites of amazingness! It's easy, isn't it? air fryers make cooking effortless, convenient and most importantly – healthy and delicious! Thanks to the revolutionary hot air technology and air-tight, compact design, air fryers cook foods evenly from all angles, producing that crunchy exterior and juicy, moist interior. Your air fryer is capable of performing a variety of cooking techniques and kitchen tasks. It can fry, roast, bake, and broil a wide variety of foods, from veggies and eggs to meats, casseroles, and desserts.

Air Fry – air frying foods is one of the most popular functions this magical kitchen gadget can perform. Unlike other frying techniques, such as deep-frying, stir-frying, or shallow frying, you do not need to preheat the pan; it will heat up quickly. Using a small amount of oil will result in a crunchy outside with a melt-in-your-mouth inside, producing loads of flavour. It's all about the timing and good preparation. For an even crispier exterior, brush the food lightly with cooking spray. It will help distribute the heat more evenly and effectively, as well as impart a succulent flavour.

Bake – From meats and pizza to delicate baked goods such as pastry and cupcakes, your air fryer can do it all! It uses a fan that circulates hot air to help food cook faster and brown evenly. Remember, your air fryer should be preheated first for most baked goods. You can toast English muffins, bread, and sandwiches in the air fryer, and this is a pretty straight-forward process. Place bread slices flat in a single layer in the cooking basket. Toast your bread at 190°C for approximately 5 minutes, flipping halfway through the cooking time. Top with cheese, fresh fruit, or maple syrup, and you have a delicious snack or breakfast.

Warm – Unlike a classic microwave oven, the air fryer reheats your meals evenly. For warming foods, just set your machine at approximately 150°C for up to 10 minutes. You can not only reheat fried food, but also make them crisp again.

Broil/Grill – Broiling is a cooking technique that uses extremely high temperatures and direct heat to make a fine char, similar to grilling. When it comes to definitions, both grilling and broiling can be used interchangeably. Broiling is a cinch in your air fryer. It is perfect for browning meats, poultry and seafood, and for melting toppings on casseroles and cheese on sandwiches. This is a convenient way to create a crunchy, golden-brown, and perfectly charred surface on your favourite foods. Therefore, increase the temperature and place the food closer to the heating element.

It is extremely important to keep an eye on your food as it will brown quickly. However, there is a difference between air-broiling and traditional broiling. Traditionally, you can broil your food in an oven or on a grill directly under high heat. On the other hand, air-broiling means that your food is cooked evenly on all sides, without flipping it. Surprisingly, the air-fried and air-broiled cut of meat turns out moist and succulent.

How does it look in practice? Sprinkle fully cooked food with seasoning. Lower your food onto the air fryer baking tray. Preheat the air fryer to 200°C and put the baking tray inside the chamber. Select a short amount of time, keeping an eye on the cooking. Take it out and test for doneness. That's all!

THE BEST FOODS TO PREPARE IN YOUR AIR FRYER

Before attempting the recipes, I made a short list of pantry staples so you can familiarize yourself with the air fryer and its main functions.

Vegetables

Have you ever wondered how to cook the best ever vegetable meals? How can you make them as good as professional chefs do? Cooking veggies in the air fryer isn't all that different from roasting and baking them in the oven or on your grill. Keep in mind that the air fryer cooks your food faster than a conventional oven. What I love about air-fried veggies is that you can add numerous toppings based on what you're in the mood for. It is not only perfect for cooking simple roasted vegetables, but also for more complicated dishes such as casseroles and lasagna. You can add cheese, your favourite aromatics, meat, and eggs to create one-pan meals in no time!

Vegetables are loaded with a wide variety of vitamins, such as vitamin C, vitamin A, and vitamin B-complex. They are also an excellent source of minerals, antioxidants, phytochemicals, and fibre. Plus, raw vegetables contain live enzymes that can help you digest up to 60% of your food. Cooking can ruin valuable enzymes, so the way you prepare your food can impact your gut microbes. Thanks to the short cooking times, air frying is one of the best ways to cook your veggies.

Fish and Seafood

Air fryers are perfect tools for cooking delicate foods such as fish, shrimp, scallops, or crab legs. Using the right temperature is just as important as setting the perfect cooking time. Seafood cooks quickly and perfectly in the air fryer; you will know your fish is cooked when it loses its translucent appearance, and it is impossible to remove it without flaking apart.

Test shrimp and scallops with a fork at the thickest part; they should be opaque (not transparent) and slightly firm. Do not be tempted to overcook seafood; it will become tasteless, tough, and dry.

Low-fat fish, such as cod, tilapia, or flounder, may easily get dry when cooking in the regular oven. On the other hand, air fryers cook them to perfection due to short cooking times and hot air, which circulates throughout the chamber. You can also marinate the fish with a white wine, sherry wine, mustard, soy sauce, and spices.

Fish is a delicate and sophisticated food, so it can be easily ruined. The best tip I can give you is to keep it simple. After all, high-quality fish does not need a lot of add-ins; basic spices, a few drizzles of freshly squeezed lemon juice, and a little oil will do the job. You can always adjust the seasoning before serving.

Seafood is rich in protein, omega-3 fats, B vitamins, potassium, and selenium. Oily fish like salmon and tuna have been found to lower the risk of chronic disease. Omega-3 fatty acids have impressive health benefits; they can lower triglyceride levels, cholesterol levels, and blood sugar levels. The Scientific Advisory Committee on Nutrition recommends at least two portions of fish per week (based on a 2,000-calorie diet). EFSA (the European Food Safety Agency) also advises eating one to two servings of seafood a week. Salmon and vegetables traybake, fish and chips, fish pie, and tuna pasta bake are just some of the recipes you can make in your air fryer. So, dig in!

Poultry

Air fryer poultry recipes are versatile, easy, and quick to make. Make sure to cook poultry to the recommended internal cooking temperature, or until the juices run clear. Allow it to rest for approximately 10 minutes before carving and serving. Basic air-fried turkey and chicken go wonderfully with salads, rice, and on sandwiches. For the best results, look for white-to-yellow flesh, never gray and pasty with damaged packaging.

Meat

When it comes to pork, opt for firm flesh with a grayish-pink color. If you see relatively little fat, that cut is good for air frying. Since we use zero to little oil, a small amount of marbling will produce juicy and tender bites. An air fryer uses high heat and short cooking times, so it can toughen meat. Therefore, make sure to use tender, marbleized cuts or to marinate lean cuts. As for thickness, pork chops should be a minimum of 2 to 2.5 cm thick.

If you want to cook beef, look for tender beef cuts such as rib-eye, tenderloin, and top sirloin. Fillet steak is perfect for shorter cooking methods like air frying. Low-cost beef cuts with more connective tissue can jazz up your budget-friendly meals; however, good-quality marinades may help tenderize the meat and add more flavours and aromas. A good rule of thumb is use 1/2 cup of marinade for each 500 to 900 grams of meat. Always marinate meat in the fridge and never reuse the same marinade. For more flavours, use rubs (seasoning blends) for chops, ribs, roasts, and steaks.

Pork and beef mince can be cooked to perfection in your air fryer. Mixing two meats (e.g., beef and pork, or pork and turkey, gives you an ideal blend that won't dry out in your air fryer. You can also add bacon bits to the mix, as a good substitute for fat. You can cook burgers, meatloaves, minced beef Wellington, and mini meat pies in your air fryer. Ultimately, consuming undercooked meats, poultry, seafood, or eggs may increase your risk of foodborne illness. Therefore, cook the meat to the recommended safe minimum internal temperatures listed in the table below:

BEEF	Medium 65-70°C	Medium well done 70°C	Well-done 75°C
PORK	Chops Rib Roast 68°C	Pork Mince 71°C	Tenderloin 63°C
POULTRY	Chicken 75°C	Turkey 70°C	Duck 52°C
SEAFOOD	Fish 63°C	Crustaceans 62°C	

Eggs and Dairy

An air fryer is your go-to kitchen device for whipping up an easy and nutritious breakfast in a short period of time. Therefore, add eggs and cheese to your shopping list, since we will make omelets, frittatas, and cheese sandwiches in the air fryer. We will use baking pans, muffin tins, and waffle moulds to make the best pastries, desserts, and other baked goods. You can cook boiled eggs in this multifunctional device. Put the wire rack into the cooking basket, and then arrange the eggs on the wire rack. Next, cook the eggs at 130°C/270°F for 15 to 16 minutes (10 minutes for soft-boiled eggs and 12 minutes for medium-boiled eggs). Devour!

Frozen Foods

Having favourite frozen foods in your freezer can be a precious little habit during super busy days! Whether you're making store-bought fish fingers or homemade falafel from scratch, air fryers can cook frozen foods to perfection. I created an air fryer cooking chart so you can easily find cooking times and temperatures for your favourite frozen meals.

Breaded Foods

Who doesn't love that crunchy coating on their food? Fish fillets, onion rings, and buttermilk fried chicken turn out great in your air fryer; you just need to follow some basic rules. First, and foremost, do not forget to brush the bottom of the cooking basket with a little cooking oil to prevent your food from sticking. Apart from the fish fillets (e.g., sea bass, tilapia, haddock, cod, or monk fish) normally served as British fish and chips, you can batter shrimp, squid (also known as calamari), and steamed mussels. You can also make schnitzel, chicken nuggets, and chicken tacos in your air fryer. As for vegetarian and vegan options, you can batter tofu, mushrooms, soy steaks, and vegetables. Onion rings, mozzarella sticks, and fruit fritters are also good options for a fast snack or a sumptuous appetizer.

Remember, avoid using wet batter in your air fryer; it will create a mess, splattering all over the cooking basket. Food experts recommend using a standard breadcrumb breading in your air fryer. It means your food is coated with flour, followed by beaten egg mixture, and covered with dried breadcrumbs. Thanks to the rapid air circulation, while the food inside is cooking slowly, the breading is drying out, which results in crispy exterior and juicy, tender interior.

To prepare your breading station, simply combine some sort of flour such as wheat flour, cornstarch, or oat flour with spices. Next, add binding ingredients. These usually include eggs, milk, and baking powder. The last coating typically consists of breadcrumbs, but many foodies and air-fryer fans use ground nuts, hard cheese such as Parmesan, crushed crackers, or breakfast cereal; it gives texture and ensures a solid, crisp surface that pairs well with dipping sauces.

Panko crumbs are a type of breadcrumbs that are made from a crustless white bread; thanks to its flaky and dry consistency, Panko absorbs less oil, producing a robust texture of your food. Whole grain breadcrumbs are a healthier option, since they contain more fiber than regular breadcrumbs. You can also make your seasoned breadcrumbs: Cut Italian bread into cubes and place them in a bowl of your food processor or a high-speed blender; add your favourite spices such as dried parsley flakes, dried thyme, dried rosemary, dried basil, onion powder, and garlic granules, and process until fine crumbs form. Arrange your crumbs on a baking tray and bake them, uncovered, at 170°C for approximately 11 minutes, until lightly browned. Let cool completely before storing and using in your favourite recipes. Keep your breadcrumbs in the cupboard or the fridge.

Oil and Butter

Brush your food lightly with cooking spray before cooking. Make sure to use unrefined monounsaturated and polyunsaturated fats. You can use oils with a high smoke point, such as olive oil, peanut oil, coconut oil, or canola oil. As for extra-virgin olive oil, the smoke point doesn't matter too much. In addition to olive oil, you can also grease the cooking basket and food with softened butter. But keep in mind that the smoking temperature of butter is about 175°C; do not use butter with high-fat foods, such as fatty fish or bacon, because it can result in too much fat. You can add a bit of melted butter to get the dry seasoning rub to stick to the meat. For the best results, pat the meat, poultry and seafood dry before adding a light layer of butter or olive oil. Then, carefully and generously coat the meat in your seasoning. Summing up, do not use too much oil because that's not the point of air frying; a tablespoon or two is fairly enough to grease food and cooking basket.

Condiments

Keeping several go-to, family-friendly condiments in your pantry can be a good safety net for basic air fryer meals. We all want to make the most of our evenings during the busy weeknights, so having a few common condiments up your sleeve can be very useful! What are the most popular condiments to use with air-fried foods? They include well-known products such as ketchup, mayonnaise, mustard, wasabi, soy sauce, fish sauce, barbecue sauce, and salsa. Tahini, Sriracha sauce, tartar sauce, and honey mustard also make a good addition to simple roasted veggies, fried chicken wings, and falafel.

8 CHEF'S TIPS YOU SHOULD KNOW

1. Overcrowding the cooking basket is the most common mistake. Some pieces will burn, and some will come out undercooked.

2. If you catch yourself flipping the food and shaking the basket frequently, you do not allow your food to get a nice sear.

3. Experimenting in the kitchen is one of the best ways to get your creative juices flowing. But as a beginner, please follow the recipe completely. And one more thing – read the manufacturer's instructions.

4. Larger ingredients usually require a slightly longer cooking time than small ingredients. You can cook one-pan meals in your air fryer; just don't add all the ingredients at once.

5. For a crunchy texture, spritz a non-stick oil all over the ingredients in the cooking basket. Let them sit for a couple of minutes, then put them into your air fryer.

6. If you do not want to use any oil in your air fryer, parchment paper and tin foil are good options; just make sure to use them according to the manufacturer's directions. On the other hand, paper towels are a big no-no!

7. There are air fryers with a built-in preheating function, but for standard versions, there's a general recommendation. When baking or broiling, allow your air fryer to preheat for about five minutes. Preheating is not necessary for air frying, reheating, and toasting.

8. Avoid making sauces in air fryers and make sure to discard a marinade before adding food to the cooking basket. The excess liquid in form of water, sauce, or marinade can spoil your food and damage the machine (as the high-speed fan tend to splatter it up all around).

HOW YOU'LL BENEFIT FROM AN AIR FRYER

Now we come to the question – Is getting an air fryer worth the investment? The following paragraphs will describe some major benefits of using an air fryer.

As easy as pie

With today's busy lifestyles, we want to cook quality and delicious meals with minimal effort. Air fryer dishes are healthy, budget-friendly, and super tasty. In general, any meal that can be cooked in a conventional, convection, or toaster oven, can be prepared in air fryers. Compared to an air fryer, a regular oven will take much longer to preheat. It is well-known that standard ovens lose quite a lot of internal temperature every time you open it up, while an air fryer will continue the cooking process immediately. These features will save you tons of time as well as your money on electricity bills!

The time is ripe

Imagine you are making everything, from breakfast and vegan dishes to appetizers and sides, without the pain of spending all day in the kitchen. In this collection, you will find many recipes that take less than 30 minutes, which is the crucial reason why I prefer my air fryer. This revolutionary machine does everything my regular oven can do, but it takes less time to preheat and cook foods; it can greatly speed up the cooking process. Air fryers are known for their versatile cooking, and it is more than just frying. In my opinion, it is more like a small convection oven than a fryer. It will save you tons of time! All you need to do is toss ingredients in the cooking basket, add spices of your choice, and let your air fryer work its magic. Once the cycle has finished, the timer will ding, so you can save yourself the stress of watching the clock and keeping a constant check. You can also double or triple these recipes and use your air fryer to reheat food during busy weeknights.

Frustration and cost-saving solution

Imagine this scenario. You will be able to whip up tasty and nutritious meals with a single touch of a button. Air fryers do just that, serving not only as an oven, but also as an efficient toaster, broiler, and fryer. An air fryer will turn your kitchen from cluttered to tidy and organized in no time!

Give old-fashioned meals a new life

When it comes to healthy eating that does not compromise flavour, an air fryer is a real game changer. I am a big fan of chips, doughnuts, burgers, and nuggets, but I am not a fan of calories and fat! That's why I didn't cook and eat fried food for a long time, until I got my air fryer. And not only that, I improved my kitchen skills and took basic dishes to the next level!

HEALTH BENEFITS OF AIR FRYING

Many studies have found that air frying has both short and long-term health benefits. It tends to preserve valuable nutrients better than conventional cooking methods by virtue of short cooking times. Unlike deep-frying, you do not use too much oil while cooking in an air fryer. If you substitute oil for hot air, you can save tons of calories and avoid the harmful effects of "bad" fats.

It is well known that trans fats and reused oil can lead to increased inflammation in the body and high LDL cholesterol levels. It is also associated with major risk factors for chronic diseases such as heart diseases and type 2 diabetes. Several large clinical studies have proven that people who consume the most trans fats had a 40% higher risk of developing type 2 diabetes. Moreover, acrylamide, a chemical that naturally occurs in certain foods during high-temperature cooking processes, can raise the risk of several types of cancer, causing cell mutations and DNA damage. Chips, crackers, deep-fried starchy foods, and baked goods contain high levels of acrylamide.

Health experts found that high intakes of saturated fats may contribute to weight gain. While a small amount of healthy "good" fats is an essential part of a well-balanced diet, trans fats can increase the risk of obesity, even when consumed in minimal quantities. Fatty fish, nuts, avocado, and olive oil are excellent sources of good fats. On the other hand, foods that contain "bad" fats include margarine, red meat, cheese, coffee creamer, baked goods, and so forth.

If you substitute hot air for oil, you can cut the fat content in your food by up to 75%! For instance, deep-frying requires a few cups of oil for each meal, while pan-frying (also known as shallow-frying) calls for adding oil to your frying pan (around 1/3 full) to stop your food from sticking. On the other hand, you will need only 1 to 2 teaspoons of oil in your air fryer – a big calorie saver!

GUIDE TO USING THIS RECIPE COLLECTION

Are you looking for easy recipes for basic meals that you can cook in your air fryer? Look no further! This collection encompasses a wide variety of no-fail air fryer recipes, from breakfast and poultry recipes to vegan options and desserts. It is meant to be your reliable guide to air fryer ovens. You will be able to create the best air fryer recipes that are quick and easy to follow, and most importantly, healthy and delicious. The ingredients used in this collection are budget-friendly and accessible; the recipes include real, wholesome food, avoiding additives and artificial compounds. Further, each recipe is accompanied by detailed step-by-step instructions, so the cooking process is straightforward. You will also find information about preparation time and cooking time, as well as nutrition information, included with each recipe. In all modesty, these recipes will revamp your cooking skills and take your meals to the next level. I have broken down the chapters by categories of meals. There are seven main categories: breakfast, poultry, meat dishes, seafood, side dishes, vegetarian & vegan, and desserts.

Choosing air frying doesn't mean skimping on flavour – quite the opposite! Thanks to this revolutionary machine, you will serve tastier versions of real fried foods than ever before! This cookbook is designed to help you revive old-fashioned, vintage recipes and recreate your favourite restaurant meals.

Who is this book intended for? I wrote this cookbook to help beginners get familiar with air frying and its advantages. Further, if you are an experienced home cook in search of sumptuous meals that do not take much time, give this cookbook a try! In fact, if you have a passion for healthy, flavourful homemade meals, this recipe collection is just right for you. Say goodbye to greasy, messy fried foods and say hello to a new experience of crunchy, healthy bites!

CHEF'S NOTES

Nutrition information is calculated using an ingredient database and should be considered an estimate. Optional ingredients are not included.

Please note that some values may be rounded.

AIR FRYER COOKING GUIDE

Keep in mind that cooking time may vary depending on the size, thickness, and overall quality of your food. These are the parameters for the amount of 400-600 grams of food. Please check if your food is done, if it is not ready yet, just set the timer for a few extra minutes.

TYPE	TEMPERATURE	TIME (Mins.)	TYPE	TEMPERATURE	TIME (Mins.)

CHICKEN

TYPE	TEMPERATURE	TIME (Mins.)	TYPE	TEMPERATURE	TIME (Mins.)
Breasts, bone in	180 C	20-22	Nuggets	200 C	6-10
Chicken wings	180 C	15-20	Whole Chicken	180 C	70-75
Game hen	200 C	20-22	Tenders	180 C	8-10
Legs	180 C	20-22	Thighs, boneless	180 C	18-20
Legs, bone in	180 C	28-30	Thighs, bone in	180 C	20-22

BEEF

TYPE	TEMPERATURE	TIME (Mins.)	TYPE	TEMPERATURE	TIME (Mins.)
Burger	180 C	13-16	Meatballs (big)	180 C	10-12
Filet Mignon	180 C	18	Ribeye	200 C	10-15
Flank Steak	180 C	15-18	Round Roast	200 C	45-55
London Broil	180 C	20-28	Sirloin Steak	200 C	9-15
Meatballs (1 inch)	180 C	7-10			

PORK AND LAMB

TYPE	TEMPERATURE	TIME (Mins.)	TYPE	TEMPERATURE	TIME (Mins.)
Bacon	200 C	5-7	Rack of Lamb	180 C	22
Bacon (thick cut)	200 C	6-10	Sausages	200 C	13-15
Lamb Loin Chops	200 C	6-10	Spare Ribs	200 C	18-25
Loin	180 C	50-55	Tenderloin	200 C	5-8
Pork Chops	190 C	12-15			

TYPE	TEMPERATURE	TIME (Mins.)	TYPE	TEMPERATURE	TIME (Mins.)

FISH

TYPE	TEMPERATURE	TIME (Mins.)	TYPE	TEMPERATURE	TIME (Mins.)
Calamari	200 C	4-5	Swordfish Steak	200 C	10-12
Fish Sticks	200 C	6-10	Tuna Steak	200 C	8-10
Fish Fillets	200 C	10-12	Scallops	200 C	5-7
Salmon Fillet	180 C	12	Shrimp	200 C	5-6
Shellfish	200 C	12-15			

VEGETABLES

TYPE	TEMPERATURE	TIME (Mins.)	TYPE	TEMPERATURE	TIME (Mins.)
Asparagus	200 C	5-7	Mushrooms	200 C	5
Beets	200 C	40	Onions	200 C	8-10
Broccoli	200 C	6	Parsnip	180 C	15
Brussels Sprouts	180 C	15	Peppers	200 C	15
Carrots	180 C	13-15	Potatoes	200 C	12
Cauliflower	200 C	12-15	Potatoes (baby)	200 C	15
Corn on the Cob	200 C	6-10	Squash	200 C	12-15
Aubergine	200 C	15	Sweet Potato	180 C	35
Fennel	180 C	15	Tomato (cherry)	180 C	20-22
Green Beans	200 C	5-7	Tomato (slices)	180 C	10
Kale	120 C	12	Courgette	200 C	10

TYPE	TEMPERATURE	TIME (Mins.)	TYPE	TEMPERATURE	TIME (Mins.)

FROZEN FOOD

TYPE	TEMPERATURE	TIME (Mins.)	TYPE	TEMPERATURE	TIME (Mins.)
Breaded Shrimp	200 C	10-12	**Cheese Stick**	180 C	8-10
Fish Fillets	180 C	14-20	**Onion Rings**	200 C	8
Fish Fingers	200 C	15	**Pot Stickers**	200 C	8-10
French Fries (thin)	200 C	9-16			

DON'T FORGET TO
GET THE
TOP RECIPES FROM
THIS BOOK AS

**A DOWNLOADABLE
PDF IN COLOUR**

FOR FREE!

*KEEP READING TO FIND OUT
HOW!*

EASY PUMPKIN TARTLETS

Thanks to its aromatic taste, pumpkin purée goes well with tangy orange juice and sweet, nutty coconut milk. You can add your favourite aromatics such as anise, vanilla, and rum extract. Eat with toppings such as whipping cream, caramel sauce, or caramelised banana.

Servings: 4

TOTAL CALORIES: 365

Fat: 15.3g; Carbs: 50.5g; Protein: 7.7g; Sugars: 9.1g; Fibre: 3.1g

INGREDIENTS

- 113g (1/2 cup) pumpkin purée (canned, without salt)
- 1 small egg, whisked
- 120ml (1/2 cup) orange juice
- 120ml (1/2 cup) coconut milk
- 15g (2 tbsp) coconut oil + more for tartlet moulds
- 200g (1½ cups) all-purpose flour
- 15ml (1 tbsp.) honey
- 4g (1 tsp.) baking powder
- 4g (1 tsp.) pumpkin spice blend

INSTRUCTIONS

1. Start by preheating your air fryer to 180°C/360°F. Brush the air fryer tartlet moulds with coconut oil.
2. In a mixing bowl, thoroughly combine all the wet ingredients. In another bowl, mix all the dry ingredients. Add the wet mix to the dry ingredients; mix until everything is well incorporated.
3. Spoon the batter into tartlet moulds and cook for about 10 minutes, until golden brown.
4. Serve warm with toppings of choice and enjoy!

KID-FRIENDLY MINI PIZZAS

This recipe may become your go-to for breakfast, lunch box, and kids' birthday parties! Filled with good proteins, these pizza bites are easy to make and fun to eat! If you want to make a vegetarian version, substitute pancetta with brown mushrooms.

Servings: 4

TOTAL CALORIES: 425

Fat: 16g; Carbs: 41.8g; Protein: 26.3g; Sugars: 5.6g; Fibre: 4.7g

INGREDIENTS

- 1 350g (12 oz.) croissants dough
- 220g (8.8 oz.) salami, chopped
- 8 olives, pitted and chopped
- 250g (1 cup) mozzarella cheese, shredded
- 4g (1 tsp.) Italian spice mix
- 230ml (1 cup) tomato sauce, for dipping

INSTRUCTIONS

1. Roll out the croissant dough.
2. Place chopped pancetta, olives, cheese, and spice mix on half of the rolls, making sure to leave 1/2-inch from the edges.
3. Roll them into the triangle shape, making sure to pinch your dough to seal the edges.
4. Cook pizza crescents in the preheated air fryer at 185°C/365°F for 10 minutes, working with batches, if needed.
5. Serve with your favourite tomato sauce on the side and enjoy!

HOT AND SPICY POLENTA SQUARES

Air-fried polenta squares are perfect for a delicious grab & go breakfast. They are fully plant-based, spicy, and flavourful. Serve warm polenta fries with yoghurt, or your favourite sauce for dipping.

Servings: 4

TOTAL CALORIES: 221
Fat: 5.5g; Carbs: 37.7g; Protein: 5.8g;
Sugars: 0.5g; Fibre: 3.2g

INGREDIENTS

- 350ml (1 ½ cups) vegetable broth
- 125g (1 cup) quick-cook polenta
- 15ml (1 tbsp.) olive oil
- 4g (1 tsp.) harissa powder
- Sea salt and ground black pepper, to taste

INSTRUCTIONS

1. In a large saucepan, bring the vegetable broth to a rapid boil. Immediately reduce the heat to a simmer and gradually stir in the polenta, olive oil, harissa, salt, and black pepper, mixing continuously to avoid lumps.
2. Let it simmer for approximately 4 minutes, until the polenta has thickened. Pour your polenta into a deep tray; allow your polenta to cool completely.
3. Once your polenta is chilled, cut it into squares, using a sharp oiled knife.
4. Air fry polenta squares at 200°C/400°F for about 30 minutes, turning them over once or twice.

SCRAMBLED EGGS WITH MUSHROOMS

Make this high-protein breakfast in your air fryer and delight your family. You can use button mushrooms, Cremini mushrooms, or any other type of brown mushrooms you have on hand.

Servings: 2

TOTAL CALORIES: 202
Fat: 14.5g; Carbs: 4.7g; Protein: 13.3g;
Sugars: 2.6g; Fibre: 1.1g

INGREDIENTS

- 4 medium eggs
- Sea salt and ground black pepper, to taste
- 15ml (1 tbsp.) butter, melted
- 1 spring onion, sliced
- 100g (1 cup) button mushrooms, sliced

INSTRUCTIONS

1. In a mixing bowl, whisk the eggs until pale and frothy; add the salt, pepper, butter, onion, and mushrooms to the bowl; stir to combine well.
2. Pour the egg mixture into a lightly greased baking tray. (You can also use cupcake cases to create egg bites.)
3. Cook scrambled eggs in the preheated air fryer at 190°C/370°F for about 15 minutes, until fluffy and yellow.

THE COMPLETE UK AIR FRYER COOKBOOK

CLASSIC EGG SANDWICH

Who doesn't love egg sandwiches for breakfast? The recipe calls for hard-boiled eggs; it will take about 11 minutes to cook soft-boiled eggs in your air fryer, and 12-13 minutes for jammy eggs.

Servings: 2

TOTAL CALORIES: 402
Fat: 21.3g; Carbs: 32.3g; Protein: 19.9g; Sugars: 8.6g; Fibre: 5.8g

INGREDIENTS

- 4 eggs
- 5ml (1 tsp.) Dijon mustard
- 30ml (2 tbsp.) mayonnaise
- 1 red bell pepper, seeded and sliced
- 1 small Persian cucumber, diced
- 1 small red onion, sliced
- Sea salt and ground black pepper, to taste
- 4 thin slices whole-grain bread

INSTRUCTIONS

1. Lower the wire rack into the air fryer cooking basket; place the eggs on the wire rack.
2. Cook the eggs at 130°C/270°F for 15 minutes, until set.
3. Transfer the eggs to an ice-cold water bath to stop the cooking process; once the eggs are chilled, peel them under cold running water; chop the eggs into bite-sized pieces.
4. Next, combine the eggs with the mayonnaise, bell pepper, cucumber, and onion; season the eggs and veggies with salt and pepper, and assemble two sandwiches.

COLOURFUL MINI FRITTATAS

These mini frittatas are eye-catching, fluffy, and delicious. The recipe is also keto-friendly and gluten-free, so everyone will be satisfied! You can experiment and add veggies of your choice.
Servings: 4

TOTAL CALORIES: 187
Fat: 15.5g; Carbs: 4.7g; Protein: 7.6g; Sugars: 2.4g; Fibre: 1.1g

INGREDIENTS

- 8 large eggs, beaten
- 60 ml (4 tbsp.) double cream
- 34.5 grams (3 slices) bacon, diced
- 1 medium tomato, diced
- 1 green bell pepper, seeded and chopped
- 4g (1 tsp.) cayenne pepper
- Sea salt and ground black pepper, to taste

INSTRUCTIONS

1. Start by preheating your air fryer to 180°C/350°F. Then, brush the sides and bottom of the tartlet moulds with non-stick cooking oil.
2. In a mixing bowl, thoroughly combine all the ingredients; mix until everything is well incorporated.
3. Scrape the mixture into the prepared tartlet moulds, and then, arrange them in the air fryer basket.
4. Cook mini frittatas in the preheated air fryer for approximately 15 minutes, until a tester (fork or wooden stick) comes out dry and clean.

BAKED FRUIT SALAD

(IN MINUTES)
PREP
10
COOK
18

If you like fruits for breakfast, then do not miss out on this amazing recipe! You can eat your pears and apples fresh, but thanks to their natural sugars, these fruits become incredibly delicious when cooked in the air fryer.

Servings: 4

TOTAL CALORIES: 217
Fat: 7.5g; Carbs: 47g; Protein: 0.6g;
Sugars: 31.1g; Fibre: 5.1g

INGREDIENTS

- 2 medium pears, cored and diced
- 2 medium apples, cored and diced
- 4g (1 tsp.) ground allspice
- 85g (1/4 cup) brown sugar
- 30ml (2 tbsp.) coconut oil
- Freshly squeezed juice of 1 medium lime

INSTRUCTIONS

1. Toss your fruit with the remaining ingredients. Place the fruits in the air fryer cooking basket.
2. Cook the fruits in the preheated air fryer at 160°C/330°F for 15 minutes, shaking the basket once or twice during the cooking time.

SPICY SMOKED BACON

(IN MINUTES)
PREP
5
COOK
7

Air-fried bacon is crispy and satisfying. Plus, the clean-up is so easy! For the best results, arrange the bacon slices in a single layer and do not forget to turn them over halfway through the cooking time!

Servings: 2

TOTAL CALORIES: 230
Fat: 17g; Carbs: 15.5g; Protein: 2.6g;
Sugars: 1.8g; Fibre: 1.2g

INGREDIENTS

- 32g (4 slices) smoked bacon
- 2g (1/2 tsp.) onion powder
- 2g (1/2 tsp). garlic granules
- 4g (1 tsp.) red pepper flakes, crushed
- 2 large bread slices

INSTRUCTIONS

1. Toss the bacon with the onion powder, garlic granules, and red pepper flakes.
2. Cook the bacon slices at 200°C/400°F for about 7 minutes.
3. Top bread slices with warm air-fried bacon and enjoy!

PORRIDGE CUPS WITH PECANS

(IN MINUTES)
PREP
5
COOK
10

Make these delicious porridge cups for breakfast to stay fit and energetic all day long! They are vegan, gluten-free, and high-fibre bites you will love. If you are going sugar-free, you can substitute sugar with agave syrup or maple syrup.

Servings: 4

TOTAL CALORIES: 154
Fat: 11.3g; Carbs: 11.8g; Protein: 2.2g; Sugars: 5.8g; Fibre: 2.3g

INGREDIENTS

- 120g (1½ cups) oatmeal
- 1 large ripe banana
- 30g (2 tbsp.) brown sugar
- 4g (1/2 tsp.) ground cinnamon
- 2g (1/2 tsp.) vanilla extract
- 1g (1/4 tsp.) ground ginger
- 60g (2.2 oz) pecans, chopped

INSTRUCTIONS

1. In a mixing bowl, thoroughly combine all the ingredients. Spoon the mixture into lightly greased cupcake cases.
2. Bake your muffins in the preheated air fryer at 200°C/395°F for about 10 minutes.

EASY SCALLION CORNBREAD

(IN MINUTES)
PREP
10
COOK
15

Who doesn't love freshly baked homemade cornbread? This recipe calls for scallions, but feel free to experiment and add jarred peppers, dried tomatoes, or olives to the batter.

Servings: 4

TOTAL CALORIES: 316
Fat: 16.4g; Carbs: 36.3g; Protein: 6.6g; Sugars: 1.9g; Fibre: 2.1g

INGREDIENTS

- 60g (1/2 cup) yellow cornmeal
- 120g (1 cup) all-purpose flour
- 4g (1 tsp.) baking powder
- 4g (1 tsp.) baking soda
- 1 large egg, whisked
- 60ml (1/4 cup) olive oil
- 120ml (1/2 cup) sparkling water
- 120ml (1/2 cup) full-fat milk
- 2 scallion stalks, chopped

INSTRUCTIONS

1. Start by preheating your air fryer to 180°C/360°F. Then brush the sides and bottom of a baking tray with 1 tablespoon of olive oil.
2. In a mixing bowl, thoroughly combine all the dry ingredients. Gradually stir in the liquid ingredients, including the reserved oil; fold in the scallions.
3. Scrape the mixture into the prepared baking tray; lower the tray into the air fryer cooking basket.
4. Bake your cornbread in the preheated air fryer for approximately 15 minutes until a toothpick comes out dry and clean.

GRANDMA'S HASH BROWNS

(IN MINUTES)
PREP
5
COOK
25

A combination of a few regular potatoes, one shallot, and an egg is all you need to start your day off right! Use floury potatoes such as King Edwards. You can add your favourite combo of fresh or dried herbs if desired!

Servings: 4

TOTAL CALORIES: 236

Fat: 4.4g; Carbs: 42.3g; Protein: 6.6g; Sugars: 4.5g; Fibre: 5.8g

INGREDIENTS

- 4 medium potatoes, peeled and grated (floury potatoes work best)
- 1 medium shallot, chopped
- 1 medium egg, beaten
- 2g (1/2 tsp.) paprika
- Sea salt and ground black pepper, to taste
- 15ml (1 tbsp.) bacon grease

INSTRUCTIONS

1. Make sure to wring out as much liquid from the potatoes as you can, using cheesecloth. (You can also use tea towels).
2. In a mixing bowl, thoroughly combine the squeezed potatoes, shallot, egg, paprika, salt, and black pepper until everything is well incorporated.
3. Brush the bottom of the air fryer cooking basket with bacon grease.
4. Now add spoonsful of the batter into the prepared air fryer cooking basket; press them slightly with a spatula.
5. Bake your hash browns at 195°C/385°F for about 13 minutes. Turn them over and cook for a further 12 minutes, until cooked through and crispy on the bottom.

BRIOCHE FRENCH TOAST

(IN MINUTES)
PREP
5
COOK
15

How about classic French toast for breakfast? Yes, please! Serve warm French toast with maple syrup, raw or canned berries, banana, or other favourite toppings.

Servings: 2

TOTAL CALORIES: 252

Fat: 12.5g; Carbs: 26.3g; Protein: 8.1g; Sugars: 3.5g; Fibre: 1.7g

INGREDIENTS

- 1 large egg
- 30ml (2 tbsp.) double cream
- 2g (1/2 tsp.) ground cinnamon
- 15g (1 tbsp.) butter, room temperature
- 4 thick slices brioche

INSTRUCTIONS

1. Begin by preheating your air fryer to 180°C/360°F.
2. Beat the eggs with double cream until frothy. Add in ground cinnamon and butter; whisk again to combine well.
3. Next, dip brioche bread slices in the beaten egg/cream mix.
4. Cook French toast for about 15 minutes, turning halfway through cooking time to ensure even cooking.

PEANUT BUTTER TOAST

(IN MINUTES)
PREP
5
COOK
5

Toast is the ultimate breakfast food! If you haven't tried air-fried toast, you are missing out! You can garnish air-fried toast with canned blackberries or raisins. Enjoy!

Servings: 1

TOTAL CALORIES: 291
Fat: 7.5g; Carbs: 50.3g; Protein: 7.1g; Sugars: 20.5g; Fibre: 4.5g

INGREDIENTS

- 2 slices whole-wheat bread
- 30g (2 tbsp.) peanut butter
- 1 small banana, sliced

INSTRUCTIONS

1. Begin by preheating your air fryer to 160°C/320°F.
2. Toast your bread for about 5 minutes.
3. Top toasted bread slices with peanut butter and banana.

PORRIDGE BITES WITH SEEDS

(IN MINUTES)
PREP
5
COOK
17

Porridge is the common food for breakfast, but how about trying it in the air fryer? You can make these healthy bites in no time and delight your family and friends!

Servings: 5

TOTAL CALORIES: 363
Fat: 16.5g; Carbs: 47.6g; Protein: 7g; Sugars: 23g; Fibre: 4.5g

INGREDIENTS

- 45g (3 tbsp.) sunflower seeds
- 45g (3 tbsp.) pumpkin seeds
- 75g (5 tbsp.) raisins
- 160g (2 cups) old-fashioned rolled oats
- 15g (1 tbsp.) multi-grain hoop cereal
- 50g (3¼ tbsp.) peanut butter
- 50g (3¼ tbsp.) butter
- 100g (1/4 cup) golden syrup

INSTRUCTIONS

1. Thoroughly combine all the ingredients in a mixing bowl until everything is well incorporated.
2. Spoon the batter into a lightly greased baking tray.
3. Bake your porridge at 180°C/350°F for about 17 minutes. Let it sit for a couple of minutes before cutting it into squares and enjoy!

3 | POULTRY

DON'T FORGET TO GET THE
TOP RECIPES FROM THIS BOOK AS

A FREE DOWNLOADABLE PDF IN COLOUR

SCAN THE QR CODE BELOW

Just follow the steps below to access it via the QR Code (the picture code at the bottom of this page) or click the link if you are reading this on your Phone / Device.

1. Unlock your phone & open up the phone's camera
2. Make sure you are using the "back" camera (as if you were taking a photo of someone) and point it towards the QR code at the bottom of the page.
3. Tap your phone's screen exactly where the QR code is.
4. A link / pop up will appear. Simply tap that (and make sure you have internet connection) and the FREE PDF containing all of the colored images should appear.

STICKY CHICKEN DRUMSTICKS

This is a simple recipe for people who do not have enough time to cook dinner during busy weeknights. These succulent and delicious drumsticks are ready in 30 minutes!

Servings: 4

TOTAL CALORIES: 215

Fat: 12.7g; Carbs: 4.9g; Protein: 18.3g;
Sugars: 4.4g; Fibre: 0.4g

INGREDIENTS

- 450g (1 lb.) chicken drumsticks
- 4g (1 tsp.) hot paprika
- 15ml (1 tbsp.) honey
- 15ml (1 tbsp.) Dijon mustard
- 15ml (1 tbsp.) olive oil

INSTRUCTIONS

1. Toss chicken drumsticks with the other ingredients in a resalable bag; toss until chicken drumsticks are well-coated on all sides.
2. Cook chicken drumsticks at 190°C/380°F for 30 minutes, shaking the basket halfway through cooking time to ensure even cooking.

ASIAN-STYLE DUCK

Missing out on poultry during busy weeknights? Well, try this air-fried duck drumettes with an Asian flair! If you do not have lemon marmalade on hand, you can substitute it with a mixture of 100 grams of honey and 5g (one teaspoon) of freshly grated ginger.

Servings: 4

TOTAL CALORIES: 266

Fat: 10.8g; Carbs: 19.7g; Protein: 21.3g;
Sugars: 15.9g; Fibre: 0.4g

INGREDIENTS

- 450g (1 lb.) duck drumettes
- 2 cloves garlic, smashed
- 15ml (1 tbsp.) soy sauce
- 20ml (2 tbsp.) rice vinegar
- Ground black pepper, to taste
- 4g (1 tsp.) red pepper flakes, crushed
- 4g (1 tsp.) sesame oil
- 100g (3.5 oz.) lemon marmalade

INSTRUCTIONS

1. Toss the duck drumettes with garlic, soy sauce, rice vinegar, black pepper, red pepper flakes, and sesame oil. Toss until they are well coated on all sides.
2. Cook the duck drumettes at 200°C/390°F for 30 minutes, turning them over halfway through the cooking time to ensure even browning.
3. Top duck drumettes with lemon marmalade. Continue to cook for a further 10 minutes.

GRANDMA'S SPICY MEATBALLS

If you are searching for something really delicious for a family lunch, keep this recipe in your back pocket. This recipe calls for ground cumin. Here's a pro-tip: toast cumin before grinding it to bring out its amazing aromas.

Servings: 5

TOTAL CALORIES: 273
Fat: 11.4g; Carbs: 13.7g; Protein: 30g;
Sugars: 0g; Fibre: 2.2g

INGREDIENTS

- 450g (1 lb.) turkey mince, 93 % lean and 7 % fat
- 150g (6 oz.) pork mince
- 100g (1 cup) porridge oats
- 2 cloves garlic, minced
- 1 medium egg, beaten
- 30ml (2 tbsp.) full-fat milk
- 4g (1 tsp.) ground cumin
- 4g (1 tsp.) coriander
- 15g (1 tbsp.) chipotle chilli paste
- Sea salt and ground black pepper, to taste

INSTRUCTIONS

1. In a mixing bowl, thoroughly combine all the ingredients. Shape the mixture into equal balls.
2. Brush the bottom of the air fryer cooking basket with nonstick cooking spray.
3. Air fry the meatballs at 180°C/360°F for 15 minutes. Shake the cooking basket halfway through the cooking time.

HOMEMADE CHICKEN NUGGETS

We all have tried chicken nuggets in restaurants, but how about a homemade version with less oil and more flavour? Try it now and thank us later!

Servings: 4

TOTAL CALORIES: 248
Fat: 7.5g; Carbs: 19.1g; Protein: 23.3g;
Sugars: 2.1g; Fibre: 1.4g

INGREDIENTS

- 450g (1 lb.) chicken tenders, cut into bite-sized pieces
- Sea salt and ground black pepper, to taste
- 1g (1/4 tsp.) cayenne pepper
- 2g (1/2 tsp.) onion powder
- 1g (1/4 tsp.) garlic powder
- 100g (1 cup) breadcrumbs, crushed
- 15ml (1 tbsp.) olive oil

INSTRUCTIONS

1. Begin by preheating your air fryer to 200°C/390°F.
2. Season the chicken tenders with salt, black pepper, cayenne pepper, onion powder, and garlic powder.
3. In a shallow bowl, thoroughly combine the breadcrumbs with olive oil. Dip chicken tenders into the breadcrumb mixture; press to adhere.
4. Cook chicken nuggets for about 12 minutes, until they are cooked through and golden brown.

CLASSIC TURKEY BURGERS

If you are sick and tired of restaurant-style beef burgers, cook homemade turkey burgers in your air fryer. They are weight-loss friendly, easy to make, and oh-so-delicious!

Servings: 5

TOTAL CALORIES: 314

Fat: 20.1g; Carbs: 7.4g; Protein: 25.4g; Sugars: 1.4g; Fibre: 1.2g

INGREDIENTS

- 670g (1½ lb.) turkey mince, (85% lean, 15% fat)
- 30g (1/3 cup) instant oats
- 1 medium onion, chopped
- 2 garlic cloves, crushed
- 1 whole egg, beaten
- 4g (1 tsp.) fresh parsley, chopped
- Sea salt and ground black pepper, to taste
- 5ml (1 tsp.) olive oil

INSTRUCTIONS

1. Thoroughly combine all the ingredients in a mixing bowl. Shape the mixture into 5 equal patties.
2. Brush the bottom of the air fryer cooking basket with nonstick cooking oil.
3. Air fry turkey burgers at 180°C/360°F for about 15 minutes, or to your desired degree of doneness.
4. Serve warm burgers with toppings of your choice.

CREAMY CHICKEN SALAD

The taste of this recipe will make you fall in love with air-fried chicken! Other common add-ins may include celery, pickles, and a variety of greens. So good!

Servings: 4

TOTAL CALORIES: 412

Fat: 32.3g; Carbs: 5.3g; Protein: 24.7g; Sugars: 2.5g; Fibre: 1.4g

INGREDIENTS

- 450g (1 lb.) chicken breasts, boneless and skinless
- 5ml (1 tsp.) olive oil
- 1 bell pepper, seeded and chopped
- 1 small red onion, thinly sliced
- 45g (1/4 cup) green olives, pitted and sliced
- 100g (7 tbsp.) mayonnaise
- 15ml (1 tbsp.) Dijon mustard
- 10ml (2 tsp.) freshly squeezed lemon juice
- Sea salt and ground black pepper, to taste
- 226g (1 cup) iceberg lettuce, shredded

INSTRUCTIONS

1. Pat the chicken dry using tea towels. Toss the chicken breasts with olive oil.
2. Cook the chicken at 190°C/380°F for about 20 minutes, turning them over halfway through the cooking time.
3. Cut the chicken breast into strips. Then, combine the chicken with the remaining ingredients.
4. Serve well-chilled and enjoy!

BUTTERMILK CHICKEN LEGS

(IN MINUTES)
PREP 5
COOK 22

Make famous buttermilk chicken in your air fryer and surprise your taste buds! As for the coating, you can also use your favourite herbs, such as parsley, cilantro, or oregano.

Servings: 4

TOTAL CALORIES: 484
Fat: 22g; Carbs: 43.2g; Protein: 26.2g; Sugars: 3.6g; Fibre: 1.6g

INGREDIENTS

- 450g (1 lb.) chicken legs
- Sea salt and ground black pepper, to taste
- 250ml (1 cup) buttermilk
- 200g (1 1/6 cups) all-purpose flour
- 4g (1 tsp.) garlic powder
- 2g (1/2 tsp.) onion powder
- 10ml (2 tsp.) olive oil

INSTRUCTIONS

1. In a glass or ceramic bowl, place chicken legs with the salt, black pepper, and buttermilk until well coated on all sides. Cover the bowl and let it chill in your fridge overnight. Discard the marinade.
2. In another shallow bowl, mix the flour, garlic powder, and onion powder. Now, dip the chicken in the flour mixture, making sure they are well coated on all sides.
3. Brush the prepared chicken legs and the bottom of the cooking basket with olive oil; arrange them in the air fryer cooking basket.
4. Air fry the chicken legs at 180°C/365°F for 22 minutes, flipping them halfway through cooking time to ensure even cooking.

TURKEY BREASTS WITH BACON

(IN MINUTES)
PREP 5
COOK 25

Have you ever tried turkey in your air fryer? Here is the best recipe for melt-in-your-mouth turkey breasts with a well-browned surface and tender inside. Perfect!

Servings: 4

TOTAL CALORIES: 299
Fat: 12g; Carbs: 13.3g; Protein: 31.8g; Sugars: 8.3g; Fibre: 1.6g

INGREDIENTS

- 670g (1½ lb.) turkey breast, boneless and cut into pieces
- 60g (2 oz.) rashers smoked bacon, thinly sliced
- 2 sprigs fresh rosemary, leaves chopped
- Kosher salt and freshly ground black pepper, to taste
- 4g (1 tsp.) red pepper flakes, crushed

INSTRUCTIONS

1. Pat turkey breast dry using tea towels. Then rub the turkey breast with the spices until they are well coated on all sides.
2. Cook turkey breast in the preheated air fryer at 200°C/395°F for approximately 15 minutes.
3. Turn turkey breast over, top them with bacon, and continue to cook for a further 8 to 10 minutes.
4. (Turkey is done when the internal temperature reaches 73°C/165°F).

THE COMPLETE UK AIR FRYER COOKBOOK

TURKEY THIGHS WITH SWEET ONIONS

If you cannot wait for the holidays to cook a whole bird, use your air fryer to cook a couple of turkey thighs! Season them with your favourite poultry seasoning mix and enjoy!

Servings: 4

TOTAL CALORIES: 310
Fat: 16.2g; Carbs: 0.9g; Protein: 38.4g; Sugars: 0g; Fibre: 0.3g

INGREDIENTS

- 670g (1½ lb.) turkey thighs, boneless
- 15g (1 tbsp.) bacon grease
- 15g (1 tbsp.) poultry seasoning mix
- Kosher salt and freshly ground black pepper, to taste
- 2 medium sweet onions, cut into wedges

INSTRUCTIONS

1. Pat turkey breast dry using tea towels. Then, rub the turkey thighs with bacon grease and spices until they are well coated on all sides.
2. Cook turkey thighs breast in the pre-heated air fryer at 195°C/390°F for approximately 20 minutes.
3. Turn them over, top them with sweet onions; continue to cook for a further 10 minutes.
4. (Turkey is done when the internal temperature reaches 73°C/165°F).

ITALIAN-STYLE CHICKEN CASSEROLE

Love Italian food? This casserole recipe calls for dark chicken meat, Italian mushrooms, and authentic herbs such as basil and parsley.
Servings: 4

TOTAL CALORIES:309
Fat: 17.7g; Carbs: 14g; Protein: 23.3g; Sugars: 6g; Fibre: 2.9g

INGREDIENTS

- 450g (1 lb.) chicken drumsticks, boneless and sliced into strips
- 22ml (1½ tbsp.) olive oil
- 1 small leek, finely sliced
- 2 garlic cloves, minced
- 1 large bell pepper, sliced
- 220g (1/2 lb.) Cremini mushrooms, sliced
- 110ml (1/2 cup) tomato sauce
- 15g (1 tbsp.) Italian herb mix

INSTRUCTIONS

1. Arrange the chicken strips in the bottom of a lightly greased baking tray.
2. Add the other ingredients to the baking tray; gently stir to combine.
3. Bake chicken casserole at 180°C/360°F for 30 minutes, until cooked through.

CHICKEN SAND-WICHES

(IN MINUTES)
PREP **10**
COOK **70**

Did you know that you can cook whole chicken in your air fryer? Forget bulky ovens and use your air fryer to make the best chicken sandwiches ever! Favourite add-ins include tomato, lettuce, pickles, mayo, ketchup, relish, and so on.

Servings: 6

TOTAL CALORIES: 456
Fat: 26.1g; Carbs: 21.3g; Protein: 31.6g;
Sugars: 2.6g; Fibre: 0.9g

INGREDIENTS

- 900g (2 lb.) whole chicken, giblets removed
- 4g (1 tsp.) hot paprika
- Sea salt and ground black pepper, to taste
- 4g (1 tsp.) dried parsley flakes
- 15ml (1 tbsp.) olive oil
- 6 sandwich rolls

INSTRUCTIONS

1. Toss the chicken with the other ingredients in a resalable bag; toss until the chicken is well coated on all sides.
2. Lower the chicken (breast side down) into the lightly oiled air fryer cooking basket.
3. Cook the chicken at 180°C/360°F for approximately 50 minutes.
4. Turn the chicken over and continue to cook for 20 minutes more.
5. Allow the chicken to rest for about 10 minutes on a cutting board.
6. Cut the chicken, discard the bones (and skin, if desired), and assemble your sandwiches. Use toppings of choice.

ROTISSERIE-STYLE ROAST CHICKEN

(IN MINUTES)
PREP **10**
COOK **70**

When it comes to Italian seasonings, you can use basil, thyme, marjoram, parsley, oregano, and so forth. It will take just 10 minutes of prep time, while your air fryer will do the rest!

Servings: 5

TOTAL CALORIES: 319
Fat: 23g; Carbs: 2.1g; Protein: 23.3g;
Sugars: 0.9g; Fibre: 0.3g

INGREDIENTS

- 670g (1½ lb.) whole chicken, giblets removed
- 4g (1 tsp.) Italian spice mix
- 4g (1 tsp.) red pepper flakes
- 4g (1 tsp.) fresh garlic, pressed
- Sea salt and ground black pepper, to taste
- 15ml (1 tbsp.) olive oil

INSTRUCTIONS

1. Rub the chicken with the other ingredients until it is well-coated on all sides.
2. Lower the chicken (breast side down) into the lightly oiled air fryer cooking basket.
3. Cook the chicken at 180°C/360°F for approximately 50 minutes. Turn the chicken over and continue to cook for 20 minutes more.
4. Transfer the chicken to a cutting board and leave it to rest for about 10 minutes before carving and serving.

MINI CHICKEN MEATLOAVES

(IN MINUTES)
PREP 5
COOK 15

What's better than freshly baked, juicy meatloaf? Mini meatloaves with sweet-and-sour glaze! Perfect for parties, potlucks, and family gatherings, these mini meatloaves are easy to make in the air fryer! You can eat them warm or cold; you can use leftovers to make sandwiches for dinner or breakfast.

Servings: 6

TOTAL CALORIES:192

Fat: 8.4g; Carbs: 9g; Protein: 20.2g;
Sugars: 4.1g; Fibre: 0.6g

INGREDIENTS

- 450g (1 lb.) chicken mince
- 150g (6 oz.) pork mince (96% lean, 4% fat)
- 50g (2 oz.) fresh breadcrumbs
- 1 medium egg, beaten
- 2 cloves garlic, minced
- 2 spring onions, sliced
- Sea salt and ground black pepper, to taste
- 15ml (1 tbsp.) tomato purée
- 4g (1 tsp.) ground cumin
- 4g (1 tsp.) Dijon mustard
- 15ml (1 tbsp.) honey
- 15g (1 tbsp.) paprika (optional)

INSTRUCTIONS

1. In a mixing bowl, thoroughly combine the minced meat, breadcrumbs, egg, garlic, onions, salt, and black pepper. Scrape the mixture into lightly oiled muffin cases.
2. Lower the muffin cases into the air fryer cooking basket.
3. Air fry mini meatloaves at 180°C/360°F for 10 minutes.
4. In a small mixing bowl, thoroughly combine the tomato purée, ground cumin, mustard, honey, and paprika (if using). Spread the mixture on the top of each muffin and continue baking for a further 5 minutes, until the centre of each meatloaf reaches 74°C/165°F.

LOADED TURKEY FRITTATA

(IN MINUTES)
PREP 5
COOK 15

Love Italian frittata? Here is the perfect recipe for you to try in your air fryer! This easy-to-follow recipe is endlessly adaptable, so you can add your favourite fixings, such as veggies, cheese, dried tomatoes, olives, and so forth.

Servings: 4

TOTAL CALORIES:308

Fat: 21.3g; Carbs: 4.7g; Protein: 24.2g;
Sugars: 1.4g; Fibre: 0.5g

INGREDIENTS

- 8 large eggs, beaten
- 60g (4 tbsp.) double cream
- 200g (3 slices) turkey mince
- 1 green bell pepper, seeded and chopped
- 4g (1 tsp.) red pepper flakes
- 4g (1 tsp.) dried basil
- 60g (4 tbsp.) goat cheese, at room temperature, crumbled
- Sea salt and ground black pepper, to taste

INSTRUCTIONS

1. Start by preheating your air fryer to 180°C/350°F. Then brush a baking tray with nonstick cooking oil.
2. In a mixing bowl, thoroughly combine all the ingredients; mix until everything is well incorporated.
3. Scrape the mixture into the prepared baking tray, and then lower it into the air fryer basket.
4. Cook your frittata in the preheated air fryer for approximately 15 minutes or until a tester (fork or wooden stick) comes out dry and clean.

CHICKEN WRAPS

(IN MINUTES)
PREP
5
COOK
25

Packed with wholesome ingredients, these chicken wraps make a healthy choice for a family dinner. Flatbreads and whole-wheat tortillas also work well in this recipe.

Servings: 4

TOTAL CALORIES: 452
Fat: 30g; Carbs: 19.2g; Protein: 27.1g;
Sugars: 2.7g; Fibre: 1.7g

INGREDIENTS
- 450g (1 lb.) chicken breasts, boneless and skinless
- 5ml (1 tsp) olive oil
- 1 small Persian cucumber, thinly sliced
- 1 small red onion, thinly sliced
- 100g (7 tbsp.) mayonnaise
- 30g (2 tbsp.) yellow mustard
- Sea salt and ground black pepper, to taste
- 1 cup (8 oz.) iceberg lettuce, shredded
- 4 medium pita breads

INSTRUCTIONS
1. Pat the chicken dry using tea towels. Toss the chicken breasts with olive oil.
2. Cook the chicken at 190°C/380°F for about 20 minutes, turning them over halfway through the cooking time.
3. Shred the chicken breasts using two forks.
4. Assemble your wraps. Place wraps on a board; add the shredded chicken, along with the other ingredients; roll them up and warm your wraps in the air fryer at 160°C/320°F for about 5 minutes.

4 | MEAT

DON'T FORGET TO GET THE

TOP RECIPES FROM THIS BOOK
AS

A FREE DOWNLOADABLE PDF IN COLOUR

SCAN THE QR CODE BELOW

Just follow the steps below to access it via the QR Code (the picture code at the bottom of this page) or click the link if you are reading this on your Phone / Device.

1. Unlock your phone & open up the phone's camera
2. Make sure you are using the "back" camera (as if you were taking a photo of someone) and point it towards the QR code at the bottom of the page.
3. Tap your phone's screen exactly where the QR code is.
4. A link / pop up will appear. Simply tap that (and make sure you have internet connection) and the FREE PDF containing all of the colored images should appear.

STRIP STEAK WITH BLUE CHEESE BUTTER

(IN MINUTES)
PREP
5
COOK
18

Make a sophisticated and delicious lunch in under 20 minutes in your air fryer! While your steak is cooking, you can make the best topping ever, mixing blue cheese, butter, and garlic. Minimal work with great results!

Servings: 4

TOTAL CALORIES: 367
Fat: 23.9g; Carbs: 1.6g; Protein: 37.3g;
Sugars: 0.8g; Fibre: 0.3g

INGREDIENTS

- 670g (1½ lb.) strip steaks
- 4g (1 tsp.) red pepper flakes crushed
- Sea salt and ground black pepper, to taste
- 5ml (1 tsp.) olive oil

Blue Cheese Butter:
- 30g (2 oz.) blue cheese, crumbled
- 30g (2 oz.) butter, softened
- 4g (1 tsp) fresh garlic, crushed

INSTRUCTIONS

1. Toss strip steaks with the spices and olive oil until all sides are well coated; transfer the steaks to the lightly greased air fryer cooking basket.
2. Cook the steaks at 180°C/365°F for 15 to 18 minutes, or to your desired degree of doneness; make sure to turn them over halfway through the cooking time.
3. While the steaks are cooking, mix the cheese, butter, and garlic in a small mixing bowl. Serve warm steaks, dolloped with the blue cheese butter.

ELEGANT DIJON CHUCK

(IN MINUTES)
PREP
10
COOK
17

Top chuck steak, also known as the flat iron steak, is a perfect cut of beef for cooking in air fryer. It always turns out great, succulent, and full of flavour.

Servings: 3

TOTAL CALORIES: 249
Fat: 11.5g; Carbs: 2.1g; Protein: 32.4g;
Sugars: 0.8g; Fibre: 0.8g

INGREDIENTS

- 450g (1 lb.) top chuck steak
- 5ml (1 tbsp.) Dijon mustard
- Sea salt and ground black pepper, to taste
- 4g (1 tsp.) cayenne pepper
- 2g (1/2 tsp.) dried rosemary
- 10ml (2 tsp.) olive oil

INSTRUCTIONS

1. Toss top chuck with the remaining ingredients in a Ziploc bag; shake to coat well and allow it to marinate for at least 2 hours.
2. Next, preheat your air fryer to 180°C/365°F. Brush the bottom of the air fryer cooking basket with nonstick cooking spray.
3. Cook the marinated top chuck in the preheated air fryer for approximately 17 minutes. Let it rest for approximately 10 minutes before carving and serving.

FESTIVE LONDON BROIL

(IN MINUTES)
PREP
5
COOK
28

London broil, also known as a top round roast, is a tough cut of meat; if you tend to prepare it correctly, do not forget to marinate it for about 2 hours before being cooked. On the other hand, it has a low-fat content, so it will be perfect for keto diet or any other weight loss diet.

Servings: 5

TOTAL CALORIES: 326

Fat: 17.8g; Carbs: 0.4g; Protein: 41.2g;
Sugars: 0.4g; Fibre: 0.1g

INGREDIENTS

- 670g (1½ lb.) London broil
- 30ml (2 tbsp.) olive oil
- 60ml (1/4 cup) dry red wine
- 5ml (1 tsp.) Dijon mustard
- 4g (1 tsp.) garlic, crushed
- 1 bay leaf
- 1 rosemary sprig
- 4g (1 tsp.) smoked paprika
- Sea salt and ground black pepper, to taste

INSTRUCTIONS

1. In a ceramic or glass dish, place London broil, olive oil, wine, mustard, garlic, leaf, rosemary, paprika, salt, and black pepper; let it marinate for 2 hours in your fridge.
2. Cook London broil in the preheated air fryer at 180°C/360°F for 14 minutes.
3. Now, lightly brush London broil with the reserved marinade, turn it over, and continue to cook for a further 14 minutes.
4. Slice the cooked London broil against the grain.

PERFECT ROAST BEEF

(IN MINUTES)
PREP
5
COOK
45

Let the beef come to room temperature before you want to cook it. Once cooked, take the basket out of the air fryer and transfer the roast beef to a board; leave it to rest for approximately 10 minutes before carving.

Servings: 4

TOTAL CALORIES: 373

Fat: 25.9g; Carbs: 1.6g; Protein: 32.9g;
Sugars: 0.6g; Fibre: 0.2g

INGREDIENTS

- 670g (1½ lb.) beef roast (topside of beef)
- 10ml (2 tsp.) olive oil
- 4g (1 tsp.) sage
- 4g (1 tsp.) thyme
- 4g (1 tsp.) rosemary
- Sea salt and ground black pepper, to taste
- 2 medium carrots, cut into rounds
- 2 sticks celery, peeled and diced
- 1 bulb of garlic, break it into cloves, unpeeled

INSTRUCTIONS

1. Rub beef roast with olive oil, herbs, salt, and black pepper; now, place the beef in the air fryer cooking basket.
2. Cook the beef roast in your air fryer at 185°C/365°F for 30 minutes. Turn the beef over and top it with carrots, celery, and garlic; continue to cook the beef for a further 15 minutes.
3. Cover the warm roast beef with tin foil and a tea towel, and let it rest for about 10 minutes before carving and serving.

RESTAURANT-STYLE PULLED PORK

This classic restaurant-style dish uses coriander seeds, garlic paste, and barbecue sauce for its distinctive taste. To make a garlic paste, puree peeled garlic with a bit of oil in your food processor until smooth.

Servings: 4

TOTAL CALORIES: 392
Fat: 24.7g; Carbs: 10g; Protein: 30.4g;
Sugars: 7.3g; Fibre: 0.5g

INGREDIENTS

- 450g (1 lb.) pork shoulder, boneless and trimmed of excess fat
- 15ml (1 tbsp.) olive oil
- 4g (1 tsp.) coriander seeds
- Sea salt and ground black pepper, to taste
- 60ml (1/4 cup) barbecue sauce
- 4g (1 tsp.) garlic paste

INSTRUCTIONS

1. Toss pork shoulder with the other ingredients until it is well coated on all sides.
2. Cook pork shoulder in the preheated air fryer at 180°C/360°F for 50 to 55 minutes. Make sure to turn pork shoulder once or twice to ensure during the cooking time.
3. You can also brush it with some extra barbecue sauce.
4. Let it rest on a board for about 10 minutes. After that, shred the pork shoulder with two forks.
5. Serve with hot orzo or brown rice and enjoy!

EASY RUMP STEAK

Rump steak is one of the highest-quality cuts of beef available. When it comes to aromatics, season rump steak generously with sea salt and black pepper. Rosemary, thyme, and tarragon are good options too.

Servings: 4

TOTAL CALORIES: 244
Fat: 10.2g; Carbs: 0.6g; Protein: 36.2g;
Sugars: 0.2g; Fibre: 0.3g

INGREDIENTS

- 670g (1½ lb.) rump steak
- 15ml (1 tbsp.) Dijon mustard
- 15ml (1 tbsp.) olive oil
- 4g (1 tsp.) beef seasoning mix
- Kosher salt and ground black pepper, to taste

INSTRUCTIONS

1. Pat the steaks dry using tea towels.
2. Toss your steak with the other ingredients until it is well-coated on all sides.
3. Cook the steaks at 180°C/365°F for 15 to 18 minutes, or to your desired degree of doneness; make sure to turn them over halfway through the cooking time.

HERBED LOIN ROAST

Make sure to take the pork loin out of your fridge for about 1 hour before cooking. The recipe calls for dried rosemary and basil, but feel free to use your favourite aromatics, both fresh and dried.

Servings: 4

TOTAL CALORIES: 389
Fat: 22g; Carbs: 0.1g; Protein: 42.5g;
Sugars: 0g; Fibre: 0.1g

INGREDIENTS

- 670g (1½ lb.) pork loin
- Sea salt and ground black pepper, to taste
- 2g (1/2 tsp.) cayenne pepper, or more to taste
- 15g (1 tbsp.) dried rosemary
- 15g (1 tbsp.) dried basil
- 5ml (1 tsp.) olive oil

INSTRUCTIONS

1. Pat dry pork loin using tea towels; then, toss the pork with the other ingredients until it is well coated on all sides.
2. Cook pork loin in the preheated air fryer at 185°C/365°F for 55 minutes (for medium/well done), turning over halfway through the cooking time.
3. If the internal temperature reads 70°C/160°F, let the pork loin rest for 5 minutes before slicing.
4. Slice the pork into smaller pieces and enjoy!

CRISPY PORK BELLY

You will need just 4 common ingredients to make pork belly with a golden-brown crackling and succulent, juicy interior. Pork belly is a perfect food for the air fryer!

Servings: 5

TOTAL CALORIES: 477
Fat: 48.2g; Carbs: 1.1g; Protein: 8.7g;
Sugars: 0.6g; Fibre: 0.2g

INGREDIENTS

- 450g (1 lb.) pork belly, boneless and sliced into pieces
- 4g (1 tsp.) hot paprika
- 15ml (1 tbsp.) soy sauce
- Sea salt and ground black pepper, to taste

INSTRUCTIONS

1. Toss the pork belly with the other ingredients.
2. Cook the pork belly in the preheated air fryer at 200°C/400°F for 25 minutes; turn it over, reduce the heat to 160°C/320°F, and continue to cook for a further 30 minutes.
3. Let it rest on a board for approximately 10 minutes before carving and serving.

PAPRIKA PORK CHOPS

For this recipe, you can use blade chops or sirloin chops. Good seasonings for pork chops include ground cumin, chilli powder, garlic, and thyme.

Servings: 5

TOTAL CALORIES: 309
Fat: 17.2g; Carbs: 0.3g; Protein: 35.1g;
Sugars: 0.2g; Fibre: 0.2g

INGREDIENTS

- 670g (1½ lb.) pork chops (1/2-inch thick)
- 15ml (1 tbsp.) olive oil
- 4g (1 tsp.) hot paprika
- 4g (1 tsp.) dried parsley flakes
- Sea salt and ground black pepper, to taste

INSTRUCTIONS

1. Using a resealable bag, toss pork chops with the remaining ingredients.
2. Cook pork chops in the preheated air fryer at 190°C/380°F for 12 to 15 minutes; until cooked through.
3. Serve warm and enjoy!

EASY GREEK-STYLE GYRO

Roasting Boston butt, as a part of the pork shoulder, in the air fryer is a real game changer! It is simple, quick, and effortless. If you prefer Boston butt with amazing, extra-crispy crackling, this recipe will fit the bill!

Servings: 4

TOTAL CALORIES:207
Fat: 11.2g; Carbs: 0.4g; Protein: 24.8g;
Sugars: 0.2g; Fibre: 0.4g

INGREDIENTS

- 450g (1 lb.) Boston butt, boneless and excessive fat removed, cut into bite-sized cubes
- 2g (1/2 tsp.) garlic powder
- 2g (1/2 tsp.) onion powder
- 2g (1/2 tsp.) cumin powder
- 2g (1/2 tsp.) dried oregano
- 4g (1 tsp.) cayenne pepper
- Sea and ground black pepper, to taste
- 15ml (1 tbsp.) olive oil

INSTRUCTIONS

1. Place Boston butt with the remaining ingredients in a resealable bag. Now, give it a good shake until Boston butt is well coated with spices.
2. Cook Boston butt at 180°C/360°F for 50 to 55 minutes, depending on its thickness; make sure to flip the pork once or twice during the cooking time.
3. After that, shred the pork with two forks and serve on the warmed pita bread with add-ins and toppings of choice. They include tzatziki, tomatoes, red onion, mayo, cucumber, and so forth.

PERFECTLY COOKED SAUSAGE

Use your air fryer to cook pork sausage without the need for additional grease! Set your machine to 180 degrees C and 13 minutes to make perfectly cooked sausages every time! Serve warm sausages in sandwich buns and enjoy!

Servings: 4

TOTAL CALORIES: 388
Fat: 35.2g; Carbs: 0.7g; Protein: 16.3g; Sugars: 0g; Fibre: 0.1g

INGREDIENTS

- 450g (1 lb.) pork sausages

INSTRUCTIONS

1. Pierce the sausages all overusing a sharp knife.
2. Arrange the sausages in the air fryer cooking basket.
3. Air fry your sausages at 185°C/365°F for about 12 minutes, shaking the basket halfway through the cooking time.

STICKY SPARERIBS

If you want ribs for dinner but you do not have time to cook, this recipe will fit the bill! Once spareribs are cooked, place them on a paper towel; this trick will help them to reabsorb flavours and juices.

Servings: 4

TOTAL CALORIES: 388
Fat: 35.2g; Carbs: 0.7g; Protein: 16.3g; Sugars: 0g; Fibre: 0.1g

INGREDIENTS

- 450g (1 lb.) spareribs
- 15ml (1 tbsp.) Dijon mustard
- 235g (1 cup) tomato ketchup
- 4g (1 tsp.) brown sugar
- 30ml (2 tbsp.) Worcestershire sauce
- Sea salt and ground black pepper, to taste

INSTRUCTIONS

1. Toss spareribs with the remaining ingredients until well coated on all sides.
2. Arrange the ribs in the air fryer cooking basket.
3. Air fry spareribs at 180°C/360°F for about 25 minutes, shaking the basket halfway through the cooking time.

EASY PORK KABOBS

Do not forget to soak bamboo skewers for about 30 minutes before cooking (otherwise, they can burn up quickly). Serve the pork kabobs with dipping sauce on the side.

Servings: 4

TOTAL CALORIES: 253
Fat: 10.2g; Carbs: 0.5g; Protein: 36.9g; Sugars: 0.2g; Fibre: 0.2g

INGREDIENTS

- 670g (1½ lb.) pork tenderloin, cut into bite-sized pieces
- 70g (2.5 oz.) bacon, cut into pieces
- 1 small courgette, sliced
- 15ml (1 tbsp.) yellow mustard
- 2g (1/2 tsp.) cayenne pepper, or more to taste
- Sea salt and ground black pepper, to taste

INSTRUCTIONS

1. Pat dry pork tenderloin using tea towels; toss pork tenderloin, bacon, and courgette with the mustard, cayenne pepper, salt, and black pepper.
2. Thread the pork, bacon, and courgette onto bamboo skewers.
3. Cook pork kabobs in the preheated air fryer at 200°C/395°F for 12 minutes (for medium/well done), turning them over halfway through the cooking time.

CHEESY MEATBALL SLIDERS

Air fryer sliders are a real game changer! They are juicy, flavourful, and kid-friendly. Double or triple the recipe for a birthday party and serve your sliders with mini cornichons, if desired.

Servings: 4

TOTAL CALORIES: 433
Fat: 23.2g; Carbs: 23.7g; Protein: 29.3g; Sugars: 4.1g; Fibre: 1.4g

INGREDIENTS

- 225g (1/2 lb.) pork mince
- 225g (1/2 lb.) beef mince
- 30g (1/4 cup) cheddar cheese, shredded
- 15ml (1 tbsp.) yellow mustard
- 2g (1/2 tsp.) red pepper flakes
- Sea salt and ground black pepper, to taste
- 4 mini rolls

INSTRUCTIONS

1. In a mixing bowl, thoroughly combine all the ingredients. Shape the mixture into equal balls.
2. Brush the bottom of the air fryer cooking basket with nonstick cooking spray.
3. Air fry the meatballs at 180°C/360°F for 15 minutes. Shake the cooking basket halfway through the cooking time.
4. Place your meatballs on mini rolls and serve with some extra yellow cheese, if desired.

5 | FISH & SEAFOOD

DON'T FORGET TO GET THE
TOP RECIPES FROM THIS BOOK
AS

A FREE DOWNLOADABLE PDF IN COLOUR

SCAN THE QR CODE BELOW

Just follow the steps below to access it via the QR Code (the picture code at the bottom of this page) or click the link if you are reading this on your Phone / Device.

1. Unlock your phone & open up the phone's camera
2. Make sure you are using the "back" camera (as if you were taking a photo of someone) and point it towards the QR code at the bottom of the page.
3. Tap your phone's screen exactly where the QR code is.
4. A link / pop up will appear. Simply tap that (and make sure you have internet connection) and the FREE PDF containing all of the colored images should appear.

EASY CAJUN SHRIMP

Are you looking for an easy recipe for a delicious weeknight dinner? Look no further! This Cajun shrimp recipe is full of flavour and simple to put together with minimal hands-on time!

Servings: 3

TOTAL CALORIES: 174
Fat: 5.4g; Carbs: 1.1g; Protein: 30.4g; Sugars: 0.4g; Fibre: 0.1g

INGREDIENTS

- 450g (1lb.) shrimp, peeled and deveined
- 15ml (1 tbsp.) olive oil
- 1 small lemon, freshly juiced
- 4g (1 tsp.) Cajun spice mix

INSTRUCTIONS

1. In a resealable bag, toss shrimp with the other ingredients; transfer them to the air fryer cooking basket.
2. Cook shrimp in the preheated air fryer at 200°C/400°F for 3 minutes; shake the basket and cook for 3 minutes longer.
3. Taste and adjust the seasonings.

FISH AND CHIPS

Do not forget to pat the fish dry; in fact, paper or tea towels will absorb the water content and ensure a crispy coating.

Servings: 4

TOTAL CALORIES: 254
Fat: 6.2g; Carbs: 22.5g; Protein: 26.5g; Sugars: 0.6g; Fibre: 2.5g

INGREDIENTS

- 10ml (2 tsp.) olive oil
- 225g (1/2 lb.) potatoes, peeled and cut into chips
- 450g (1 lb.) grouper fillets
- 1 medium egg, beaten
- Sea salt and ground black pepper, to taste
- 70g (1/2 cup) oat flour
- 4g (1 tsp.) Old Bay seasoning

INSTRUCTIONS

1. Toss potato chips with 5ml (1 tsp.) of olive oil. Air fry your chips at 190°C/390°F for about 20 minutes, shaking the basket after 20 minutes so they will cook evenly.
2. Pat the fish dry using paper or tea towels. In a shallow bowl, beat the egg with salt and pepper. In a separate shallow bowl (or plate), thoroughly combine the oat flour with Old Bay seasoning mix.
3. Dip fish fillets in the egg mixture, then coat both sides of the grouper fillets with the oat flour mixture, pressing to adhere.
4. Brush the grouper fillets with the remaining olive oil and arrange them in the air fryer cooking basket.
5. Cook the fish at 200°C/400°F for 6 minutes; flip them over and cook for a further 6 minutes, until your fish flakes easily when tested with a fork.

LEMON GARLIC SEA SCALLOPS

Dinner, please! These delicious scallops are ready in no time. Lemon and garlic work particularly well with scallops, so give this air fryer recipe a try!

Servings: 4

TOTAL CALORIES: 93
Fat: 1.7g; Carbs: 4.6g; Protein: 13.8g; Sugars: 0.2g; Fibre: 0.3g

INGREDIENTS

- 450g (1 lb.) jumbo sea scallops, cleaned and patted dry
- 30ml (2 tbsp.) lemon juice, freshly squeezed
- 2 garlic cloves, crushed
- Sea salt ground black pepper, to taste
- 10ml (2 tsp.) extra-virgin olive oil
- 5ml (1 tsp.) Dijon mustard
- 4g (1 tsp.) capers, finely chopped

INSTRUCTIONS

1. Toss jumbo scallops with the other ingredients until they are well coated on all sides.
2. Cook jumbo scallops in the preheated air fryer at 200°C/400°F for 4 minutes; turn them over and cook for a further 3 minutes, until cooked through.

HOMEMADE FISH FINGERS

Try a healthier version of your favourite fast food. Salmon is loaded with protein, omega-3 fatty acids, selenium, potassium, and B vitamins.

Servings: 4

TOTAL CALORIES: 252
Fat: 7.7g; Carbs: 16.5g; Protein: 27.2g; Sugars: 1g; Fibre: 1g

INGREDIENTS

- 450g (1 lb.) salmon, skin off, pin-boned, cut into strips
- 1 large egg
- 50g (1/4 cup) all-purpose flour
- 50g (1/2 cup) fresh breadcrumbs
- 4g (1 tsp.) dried parsley flakes
- Sea salt and ground black pepper, to taste
- 5ml (1 tsp.) olive oil

INSTRUCTIONS

1. Pat the fish dry with paper or tea towels.
2. Prepare the breading station: Whisk the eggs and flour in a shallow dish (or plate).
3. Add the breadcrumbs, along with the seasonings, to a separate dish (or plate); stir to combine well.
4. Dip the fish pieces in the batter, then roll them over the breadcrumb mixture. Transfer the battered fish strips to the air fryer cooking basket and brush them with olive oil.
5. Cook the battered fish strips in the preheated air fryer at 200°C/400°F for 12 to 13 minutes, turning them over halfway through to ensure even browning.

SALMON STEAKS WITH HORSERADISH SAUCE

Cook salmon steak in your air fryer and serve it with horseradish sauce (homemade or store-bought). It is perfect for a midweek meal or romantic dinner with a beloved one!

Servings: 4

TOTAL CALORIES: 190
Fat: 8.5g; Carbs: 3.1g; Protein: 23.4g; Sugars: 1.8g; Fibre: 0.7g

INGREDIENTS

- 450g (1 lb.) salmon steak
- 30ml (2 tbsp.) dry white wine
- 4g (1 tsp.) garlic, crushed
- 15ml (1 tbsp.) olive oil
- Sea salt and ground black pepper, to taste
- 60ml (4 tbsp.) horseradish sauce

INSTRUCTIONS

1. Pat the salmon dry with paper (tea) towels.
2. Toss the salmon with the remaining ingredients. Transfer the salmon to the air fryer cooking basket.
3. Cook the salmon at 200°C/400°F for 6 minutes; turn the salmon over and continue to cook for a further 6 minutes, until opaque.

CREAMY FISH SALAD

Grilled cod and fresh veggies come together in one super-healthy and delicious salad! It would be great if you could find a good-quality mayo for this recipe.

Servings: 4

TOTAL CALORIES: 262
Fat: 16.2g; Carbs: 7.1g; Protein: 21.4g; Sugars: 1.5g; Fibre: 0.7g

INGREDIENTS

- 450g (1 pound) cod fillets
- 15g (1 tbsp.) Old Bay seasoning
- Sea salt and ground black pepper, to taste
- 15ml (1 tbsp.) olive oil
- 1 stalk celery, sliced
- 1 small red onion, sliced
- 60g (1/4 cup) mayonnaise
- 30g (2 tbsp.) corn, canned or frozen (and thawed)
- 15g (1 tbsp.) sour cream

INSTRUCTIONS

1. Pat the fish dry using paper or tea towels, then coat your fish with Old Bay seasoning, salt, black pepper, and olive oil.
2. Arrange fish fillets in the lightly greased air fryer cooking basket.
3. Cook the fish fillets at 200°C/400°F for 6 minutes; flip them over and cook an additional 6 minutes until the cod fish flakes easily when tested with a fork.
4. On a cutting board, cut the cod fish into bite-sized strips and place them in a nice, salad bowl. Add the other ingredients and gently stir to combine.

FISH BURGERS

Fish burgers are the ultimate comfort food! They are cooked in the air fryer for a lighter, healthier version of an all-time favourite.

Servings: 4

TOTAL CALORIES: 285
Fat: 4.4g; Carbs: 31.2g; Protein: 27.2g;
Sugars: 3.3g; Fibre: 1.3g

INGREDIENTS

- 40g (1/2 cup) self-raising flour
- 4g (1 tsp.) garlic granules
- 4g (1 tsp.) smoked paprika
- Sea salt and ground black pepper, to taste
- 20ml (2 oz.) cold lager
- 50g (1/2 cup) breadcrumbs
- 450g (1 lb.) pollock
- 5ml (1 tsp.) olive oil
- 4 soft rolls

INSTRUCTIONS

1. Tip the flour, garlic, paprika, salt, and black pepper into a mixing bowl. Then, pour cold lager into the bowl and mix to combine well. Place the breadcrumbs in a separate plate.
2. Dredge fish fillets through the batter. Roll them over the breadcrumbs. Brush fish burgers with olive oil and lower them into the air fryer cooking basket.
3. Cook the fish burgers at 200°C/400°F for 6 minutes; flip them over and cook an additional 6 minutes until your fish flakes easily when tested with a fork.
4. Place warm fish burgers in soft rolls and serve immediately.

HONEY DIJON SWORDFISH STEAK

If you cannot find swordfish, very good substitutes include halibut, mahi-mahi, tuna, or salmon. Honey-mustard marinade is a great way to dress up fish steak, so keep the recipe in your back pocket!

Servings: 4

TOTAL CALORIES: 190
Fat: 8.5g; Carbs: 3.1g; Protein: 23.4g;
Sugars: 1.8g; Fibre: 0.7g

INGREDIENTS

- 450g (1 lb.) swordfish steak
- 60ml (4 tbsp.) dry sherry wine
- 15ml (1 tbsp.) freshly squeezed lime juice
- 4g (1 tsp.) garlic, pressed
- 15ml (1 tbsp.) Dijon mustard
- 15ml (1 tbsp.) honey
- 15ml (1 tbsp.) olive oil
- Sea salt and ground black pepper, to taste

INSTRUCTIONS

1. Place all the ingredients in a ceramic dish; cover and let the swordfish steak marinate for at least 30 minutes in your fridge.
2. Transfer the swordfish steak to the air fryer cooking basket, reserving the marinade.
3. Cook the swordfish steak at 200°C/400°F for 6 to 8 minutes, depending on thickness.
4. Now turn the swordfish steak over and baste it with the reserved marinade; continue to cook for a further 6 minutes, until thoroughly cooked.

HALIBUT STEAK WITH COURGETTE

Courgette, also known as baby marrow, is a cinch to cook in the air fryer. This low-calorie vegetable is rich in vitamin B6, which can help you prevent chronic diseases such as diabetes and common eye disorders.

Servings: 4

TOTAL CALORIES: 233
Fat: 17.5g; Carbs: 2.3g; Protein: 17.8g;
Sugars: 0.1g; Fibre: 0.8g

INGREDIENTS

- 450g (1 lb.) halibut steak
- 225g (1/2 lb.) courgette
- Sea salt and ground black pepper, to taste
- 4g (1 tsp.) cayenne pepper
- 4g (1 tsp.) garlic granules
- 5ml (1 tsp.) olive oil

INSTRUCTIONS

1. Pat the halibut dry with paper (tea) towels.
2. Toss the halibut and courgette with the remaining ingredients. Transfer the halibut steaks to the air fryer cooking basket. Top them with courgette slices.
3. Cook the halibut at 200°C/400°F for 10 minutes; turn the halibut and courgette slices over and continue to cook for a further 10 minutes, until cooked through.

RESTAURANT-STYLE CALAMARI

Cooking fast food meals in your own kitchen can be a daunting task, but if you have your air fryer on hand, it won't be a problem. Calamari goes wonderfully with air-fried chips. Yummy!

Servings: 4

TOTAL CALORIES: 245
Fat: 6g; Carbs: 24.8g; Protein: 21.8g;
Sugars: 0.1g; Fibre: 1.1g

INGREDIENTS

- 450g (1 lb.) pound squid rings
- 1 large egg
- 70g (1/2 cup) all-purpose flour
- 50g (1/2 cup) spicy tortilla chips (taco flavour)
- 4g (1 tsp.) dried parsley flakes
- 2g (1/2 tsp.) garlic granules
- Sea salt and ground black pepper, to taste

INSTRUCTIONS

1. Pat the squid rings dry using paper (tea) towels.
2. Make the breading station: In a shallow dish, whisk the egg until pale and frothy. In another shallow dish, place the flour. In a third dish, thoroughly combine the other ingredients.
3. Dip the squid rings in the egg mixture. Then dip them in the flour. Roll squid rings over the breadcrumb mixture, coating them completely.
4. Cook your calamari at 200°C/400°F for 5 to 7 minutes, depending on the thickness of the rings.

THE COMPLETE UK AIR FRYER COOKBOOK

EASY FISH CAKES

Prepare to become totally addicted to these crispy and delicious fish cakes. Do not cook fish cakes for too long because they can turn out dry, tasteless, and dull.

Servings: 4

TOTAL CALORIES: 182
Fat: 3.6g; Carbs: 9.8g; Protein: 25.8g; Sugars: 1.7g; Fibre: 1.1g

INGREDIENTS

- 450g (1 lb.) haddock, cooked and flaked
- 1 large egg
- 60g (1 cup) breadcrumbs
- 1 garlic clove, minced
- 2 spring onion stalks, chopped
- 4g (1 tsp.) dried parsley flakes
- 4g (1 tsp.) smoked paprika
- Sea salt and ground black pepper, to taste
- 5ml (1 tsp.) olive oil

INSTRUCTIONS

1. Thoroughly combine the fish, egg, breadcrumbs, garlic, scallions, and spices in a mixing bowl.
2. Shape the mixture into small patties and place them in the lightly greased air fryer cooking basket. Brush your patties with olive oil.
3. Cook fish cakes at 185°C/365°F for about 6 minutes; turn them over and continue to cook for a further 6 minutes.

MINI FISH FRITTATAS

If you want fish, eggs, and cheese in one dish, make this frittata! The best of all – it is ready in 20 minutes! Serve with cornichons or fresh cherry tomatoes.

Servings: 4

TOTAL CALORIES: 288
Fat: 16.9g; Carbs: 4g; Protein: 27.6g; Sugars: 2.1g; Fibre: 0.5g

INGREDIENTS

- 225g (1/2 lb.) canned tuna in oil, drained
- 6 large eggs, beaten
- 60g (4 tbsp.) cream cheese
- 1 small onion, chopped
- 4g (1 tsp.) red pepper flakes, crushed
- 2g (1/2 tsp.) dried oregano
- Sea salt and ground black pepper, to taste

INSTRUCTIONS

1. Start by preheating your air fryer to 180°C/350°F. Then, brush a muffin tin with nonstick cooking oil.
2. In a mixing bowl, thoroughly combine all the ingredients.
3. Scrape the mixture into the prepared muffin tin, and then, lower it into the air fryer basket.
4. Cook mini frittatas in the preheated air fryer for approximately 15 minutes, until a tester (fork or wooden stick) comes out dry and clean.

GRILLED SHRIMP BRUSCHETTA

(IN MINUTES)
PREP **5**
COOK **11**

This is an air fryer version of the famous Italian antipasto! Top your bruschetta with grilled shrimp and delight your guests for the next cocktail party! So glam!

Servings: 4

TOTAL CALORIES: 288
Fat: 16.9g; Carbs: 4g; Protein: 27.6g;
Sugars: 2.1g; Fibre: 0.5g

INGREDIENTS

- 340g (13/4lb) shrimp, peeled and deveined
- Sea salt and ground black pepper, to taste
- 30ml (2 tbsp.) dry white wine
- 1 large garlic clove, halved
- 150g (3/4 cup) tomatoes, chopped
- 15ml (1 tbsp.) olive oil
- 4 lettuce leaves
- 4 thick slices bread

INSTRUCTIONS

1. Toss the shrimp with salt, black pepper, and wine.
2. Cook the shrimp in the preheated air fryer at 200°C/400°F for 3 minutes; shake the basket and cook for 3 minutes longer.
3. Rub bread slices with garlic, and then top them with chopped tomatoes; drizzle with olive oil and bake at 160°C/320°F for about 5 minutes.
4. Top each bruschetta with the lettuce leaf and shrimp and serve immediately.

HERB MAYO-RUBBED TUNA

(IN MINUTES)
PREP **10**
COOK **7**

Try a tuna recipe with a twist! The fish is coated with herb/mayo mixture and grilled in the preheated air fryer. This recipe is simple and delicious for an everyday meal but sophisticated enough to serve on a festive dinner.

Servings: 4

TOTAL CALORIES: 233
Fat: 17.5g; Carbs: 2.3g; Protein: 17.8g;
Sugars: 0.1g; Fibre: 0.8g

INGREDIENTS

- 450g (1 lb.) tuna steaks
- 60g (1/4 cup) mayonnaise
- 4g (1 tsp.) red pepper flakes, crushed
- 4g (1 tsp.) dried oregano
- 4g (1 tsp.) dried parsley flakes
- 2g (1/2 tsp.) dried thyme
- Sea salt and ground black pepper, to taste

INSTRUCTIONS

1. Pat the tuna steaks dry with paper (tea) towels. Mix the remaining ingredients in a small bowl.
2. Spread the top of the tuna steaks with the herb/mayo mixture. Lower the tuna steaks into the air fryer cooking basket.
3. Cook the tuna at 200°C/400°F for 6 minutes; turn the tuna steaks over and continue to cook for a further 6 minutes, until cooked through.

6 | SIDE DISHES

DON'T FORGET TO GET THE
TOP RECIPES FROM THIS BOOK
AS
A FREE DOWNLOADABLE PDF IN COLOUR

SCAN THE QR CODE BELOW

Just follow the steps below to access it via the QR Code (the picture code at the bottom of this page) or click the link if you are reading this on your Phone / Device.

1. Unlock your phone & open up the phone's camera
2. Make sure you are using the "back" camera (as if you were taking a photo of someone) and point it towards the QR code at the bottom of the page.
3. Tap your phone's screen exactly where the QR code is.
4. A link / pop up will appear. Simply tap that (and make sure you have internet connection) and the FREE PDF containing all of the colored images should appear.

SCAN ME

ROASTED STICKY BRUSSELS SPROUTS

Do you want a simple recipe for Brussels sprouts that are moist and tender inside, but caramelised and crunchy on the outside? Look no further. This recipe calls for common items you probably already have in your kitchen!

Servings: 4

TOTAL CALORIES: 98
Fat: 1.5g; Carbs: 19.5g; Protein: 4.2g; Sugars: 11.2g; Fibre: 4.5g

INGREDIENTS

- 450g (1lb.) Brussels sprouts, trimmed and halved
- 4g (1 tsp.) red pepper flakes crushed
- 2g (1/2 tsp.) onion powder
- 2g (1/2 tsp.) garlic powder
- 5ml (1 tsp.) extra-virgin olive oil
- 15ml (1 tbsp.) agave syrup
- 15ml (1 tbsp.) balsamic vinegar
- Sea salt and ground black pepper, to taste

INSTRUCTIONS

1. Toss Brussels sprouts with the remaining ingredients until they are well coated on all sides.
2. Air fry your Brussels sprouts at 180°C/360°F for 7 to 8 minutes; shake the basket and continue cooking for a further 7 to 8 minutes.

CHARRED CARROT SALAD WITH GOAT CHEESE

Pair roasted veggies with a sweet and tangy mustard sauce. Your carrots will turn out crispy, moist, and tender. Garnish them with goat cheese and enjoy!

Servings: 4

TOTAL CALORIES: 132
Fat: 5.8g; Carbs: 13.5g; Protein: 6.2g; Sugars: 6.6g; Fibre: 3.5g

INGREDIENTS

- 450g (1lb.) large carrots, trimmed
- 5ml (1 tsp.) mustard
- 15ml (1 tbsp.) sherry wine
- 5ml (1 tsp.) cumin powder
- 2g (1/2 tsp.) garlic powder
- Sea salt and ground black pepper, to taste
- 15ml (1 tbsp.) agave syrup
- 2 large handfuls arugula
- 15ml (1 tbsp.) lemon juice
- 60g (2 oz.) goat cheese, hard type, crumbled

INSTRUCTIONS

1. Halve your carrots crosswise, then quarter them lengthwise.
2. To make the mustard sauce: In a small mixing bowl, whisk the mustard, sherry wine, spices, and agave syrup.
3. Toss the carrot pieces with the sauce until they are well coated on all sides. Arrange them in a lightly greased cooking basket.
4. Air fry your carrots at 180°C/360°F for approximately 8 minutes; shake the basket and continue cooking for a further 7 to 8 minutes.
5. Add warm carrots to a nice salad bowl; top them with arugula and lemon juice; garnish with goat cheese and enjoy!

3 STREET-STYLE CORN ON THE COB

(IN MINUTES)
PREP 5
COOK 10

Corn on the cob is the ultimate Mexican street food. From now onwards, you can prepare it in your air fryer in no time!

Servings: 2

TOTAL CALORIES: 182

Fat: 12.8g; Carbs: 17.7g; Protein: 3.2g; Sugars: 3.2g; Fibre: 2.5g

INGREDIENTS

- 2 medium ears corn, shucked and halved
- 30ml (1 oz.) mayonnaise
- 2g (1/2 tsp.) garlic powder
- 4g (1 tsp.) dried parsley flakes
- 2g (1/2 tsp.) ancho chilli powder
- Flaky sea salt, to taste

INSTRUCTIONS

1. Toss the ears of corn with the remaining ingredients until they are well coated on all sides.
2. Air fry your corn at 200°C/395°F for 10 minutes, until corn kernels are tender when pierced with a knife or fork.

CAULIFLOWER STEAKS 4

(IN MINUTES)
PREP 5
COOK 12

Use your air fryer to prepare this tempting side dish in a fraction of the time! It is faster and more energy-efficient than using a regular oven.

Servings: 4

TOTAL CALORIES: 99

Fat: 4.3g; Carbs: 13.2g; Protein: 4.9g; Sugars: 5.8g; Fibre: 4.7g

INGREDIENTS

- 450g (1lb.) cauliflower, cut into small steaks
- 4ml (1 tsp.) olive oil
- 15ml (1 tbsp.) soy sauce
- 4g (1 tsp.) garlic powder
- 4g (1 tsp.) dried parsley flakes
- 5ml (1 tsp.) red pepper flakes, crushed
- Sea salt and ground black pepper, to taste

INSTRUCTIONS

1. Place the cauliflower steaks, along with the other ingredients, in a resealable bag; give it a good shake until the cauliflower steaks are well coated on all sides.
2. Air fry the cauliflower steaks at 200°C/395°F for 12 minutes, shaking the basket halfway through the cooking time.

CHEESE AND HERB-STUFFED MUSHROOMS

(IN MINUTES)
PREP
5
COOK
5

Feel free to experiment with this recipe and use another combo of herbs. You can also use medium cheddar or Swiss cheese.

Servings: 4

TOTAL CALORIES: 77
Fat: 2.5g; Carbs: 6.2g; Protein: 7.9g; Sugars: 3.2g; Fibre: 1.4g

INGREDIENTS

• 8 medium white button mushrooms, stalks removed
• 5ml (1 tsp.) olive oil
• Sea salt and ground black pepper, to taste
• 15ml (1 tbsp.) dry white wine
• 1 garlic clove, minced
• 3ml (1/2 tsp.) lemon zest, finely grated
• 30g (1 oz.) mozzarella cheese, grated
• 15g (2 tbsp.) fresh breadcrumbs (a day or two old)
• 15g (1 tbsp.) fresh parsley leaves, chopped
• 15g (1 tbsp.) fresh cilantro leaves, chopped
• 15g (1 tbsp.) fresh basil leaves, chopped

INSTRUCTIONS

1. Place the mushrooms, olive oil, salt, black pepper, and wine in a resealable bag; give it a good shake until the mushroom cups are well coated on all sides. Place the mushroom caps on a cutting board.
2. Then, make the stuffing: stir the other ingredients until everything is well combined. Divide the filling mixture between mushroom caps and arrange the mushrooms in the lightly greased air fryer cooking basket.
3. Air fry your mushrooms at 200°C/395°F for 5 minutes, until the mushrooms are cooked.

BEET SALAD WITH WALNUTS

6

(IN MINUTES)
PREP
15
COOK
40

Did you know that you can roast whole beets in your air fryer? Serve this delicious, rustic salad alongside crusty bread for a fuss-free family dinner!

Servings: 4

TOTAL CALORIES: 172
Fat: 11.3g; Carbs: 16.6g; Protein: 4.1g; Sugars: 10.6g; Fibre: 5.5g

INGREDIENTS

• 450g (1lb.) red beets, ends trimmed, peeled
• 5ml (1 tsp.) mustard
• 5ml (1 tsp.) pomegranate molasses
• 4g (1 tsp.) cumin powder
• 2g (1/2 tsp.) garlic powder
• Sea salt and ground black pepper, to taste
• 15ml (1 tbsp.) red wine vinegar
• 1 large handful mixed greens
• 60g (2 oz.) walnuts, toasted and chopped
• 1 small pack fresh herbs

INSTRUCTIONS

1. Arrange the beets in a single layer in the lightly greased air fryer cooking basket.
2. Air fry the beets at 200°C/390°F for approximately 40 minutes, shaking the basket halfway through the cooking time.
3. Let the beets cool to room temperature; then, cut your beets into thin slices and toss them with the mustard, pomegranate molasses, spices, vinegar, and mixed greens.
4. Garnish your beets with walnuts and fresh herbs.

CHICKPEA & CHEESE STUFFED TOMATOES

(IN MINUTES)
PREP
5
COOK
20

No family feast is complete without stuffed, roasted vegetables! These stuffed tomatoes go wonderfully with chicken roast, fish, and chips. Enjoy!

Servings: 3

TOTAL CALORIES: 147

Fat: 6.6g; Carbs: 17g; Protein: 6.5g; Sugars: 6.5g; Fibre: 4.5g

INGREDIENTS

- 300g (2/3 lb.) tomatoes, 3 tomatoes (scoop out and discard pulp)
- 5ml (1 tsp.) olive oil
- Sea salt and ground black pepper, to taste
- 130g (3/4 cup) canned chickpeas, drained
- 5ml (1 tsp.) red pepper flakes, crushed
- 6 olives, pitted and sliced
- 40g (1/3 cup) Feta cheese, crumbled, room temperature

INSTRUCTIONS

1. Toss your tomatoes with olive oil, salt, and black pepper. In a mixing bowl, thoroughly combine all the remaining ingredients.
2. Spoon the filling mixture into your tomatoes and arrange them in the lightly greased air fryer cooking basket.
3. Air fry the stuffed tomatoes at 180°C/360°F for about 20 minutes.

CHEESY AUBERGINE ROUNDS

(IN MINUTES)
PREP
5
COOK
10

Aubergine can help you manage blood sugar and cholesterol levels. Plus, it can help you lose weight and maintain your ideal weight. As for air-fried aubergine rounds, each serving contains only 160 kcal!

Servings: 4

TOTAL CALORIES: 160

Fat: 5.5g; Carbs: 23.7g; Protein: 4.4g; Sugars: 3.5g; Fibre: 3.3g

INGREDIENTS

- 15ml (1 tbsp.) mayonnaise
- 4g (1 tsp.) garlic granules
- 60g (1/2 cup) all-purpose flour
- 60g (1/2 cup) breadcrumbs
- 2g (1/2 tsp). dried oregano
- 30g (2 tbsp.) cheddar cheese, grated
- 300g (2/3 lb.) aubergines, thinly sliced
- 5ml (1 tsp.) olive oil
- Sea salt and ground black pepper, to taste

INSTRUCTIONS

1. Prepare the breading station. Mix the mayonnaise and garlic in a shallow dish. Place all-purpose flour in a separate shallow dish. In a third dish, thoroughly combine the breadcrumbs, oregano, and cheese.
2. Start by dipping aubergine slices in the garlic/mayonnaise; then coat them with the flour. Press them into the breadcrumb/cheese mixture, coating evenly on both sides.
3. Brush aubergine slices with olive oil; sprinkle them with salt and pepper to taste. Arrange them in the lightly greased cooking basket.
4. Air fry aubergine rounds at 190°C/370°F for 10 minutes. Serve warm and enjoy!

ROASTED BABY POTATOES

Roasted baby potatoes can be served as a side or entrée. Take baby potatoes to new heights by tossing them with fresh lemon juice, garlic, and oregano!

Servings: 4

TOTAL CALORIES: 106
Fat: 1.3g; Carbs: 21.1g; Protein: 2.6g; Sugars: 1.5g; Fibre: 2.7g

INGREDIENTS

- 450g (1 lb.) baby potatoes
- 4g (1 tsp.) garlic granules
- 2g (1/2 tsp.) dried oregano
- 5ml (1 tsp.) fresh lemon juice
- Sea salt and ground black pepper, to taste
- 5ml (1 tsp.) olive oil

INSTRUCTIONS

1. Toss baby potatoes with the remaining ingredients.
2. Cook baby potatoes at 200°C/395°F for 15 minutes, turning them over halfway through the cooking time.

ROAST PARSNIPS WITH ROSEMARY

Try this easy recipe for the best roast parsnips ever! Loaded with valuable nutrients and amazing aromas, this vegetable may become a new family favourite!

Servings: 4

TOTAL CALORIES: 106
Fat: 1.7g; Carbs: 22.3g; Protein: 2g; Sugars: 6.5g; Fibre: 5.7g

INGREDIENTS

- 450g (1 lb.) parsnip, halve them crosswise, and then, quarter them lengthwise
- 4g (1 tsp.) ground cumin
- 2g (1/2 tsp.) dried rosemary
- 4g (1 tsp.) red pepper flakes, crushed
- Sea salt and ground black pepper, to taste
- 4ml (1 tsp.) olive oil

INSTRUCTIONS

1. Toss parsnips with the remaining ingredients.
2. Cook parsnips at 180°C/360°F for 15 minutes, shaking the basket halfway through the cooking time.

THE COMPLETE UK AIR FRYER COOKBOOK

SWEET POTATO MASH WITH PE-CANS

This is the most flavourful sweet potato mash you'll ever make! Mashed, roasted sweet potatoes are topped with maple syrup and pecans for a tasty side dish that your family will love!

Servings: 4

TOTAL CALORIES: 184
Fat: 7.6g; Carbs: 27.1g; Protein: 2.5g;
Sugars: 8.1g; Fibre: 4.2g

INGREDIENTS

- 450g (1 lb.) sweet potatoes, whole
- 5ml (1 tsp.) olive oil
- 1g (1/4 tsp.) cayenne pepper
- 4g (1 tsp.) butter
- 5ml (1 tsp.) fresh lemon juice
- 14ml (1 tbsp.) maple syrup
- 30g (1/4 cup) pecans, roughly chopped

INSTRUCTIONS

1. Toss sweet potatoes with olive oil.
2. Cook sweet potatoes at 180°C/360°F for 35 minutes, shaking the basket halfway through the cooking time.
3. Mash your potatoes with cayenne pepper, butter, and lemon juice.
4. Top mashed potatoes with maple syrup and pecans. Bake mashed potatoes at 180°C/360°F for approximately 5 minutes.

BALSAMIC ROASTED ASPARAGUS

These crunchy and delicious asparagus spears are loaded with flavour from spices and bold balsamic vinegar. Plus, they are ready in 12 minutes!

Servings: 4

TOTAL CALORIES: 184
Fat: 7.6g; Carbs: 27.1g; Protein: 2.5g;
Sugars: 8.1g; Fibre: 4.2g

INGREDIENTS

- 450g (1 lb.) asparagus spears, trimmed
- 5ml (1 tsp.) olive oil
- 2g (1/2 tsp.) garlic powder
- 2g (1 tsp.) cayenne pepper
- 15ml (1 tbsp.) balsamic vinegar
- Sea salt and freshly ground black pepper, to taste

INSTRUCTIONS

1. Toss asparagus spears with the remaining ingredients.
2. Roast asparagus spears at 200°C/395°F for 7 minutes, shaking the basket halfway through the cooking time.

⑬ RANCH BROC-COLI FLORETS

These roasted broccoli florets are particularly delicious with ranch seasoning mix, a unique combo of garlic powder, onion powder, pepper, dill, parsley, salt, and dried chives

Servings: 3

TOTAL CALORIES: 67
Fat: 2.2g; Carbs: 10.5g; Protein: 4.3g; Sugars: 2.6g; Fibre: 4.2g

INGREDIENTS

- 450g (1 lb.) broccoli florets
- 2g (1 tsp.) cayenne pepper
- 1g (1/2 tsp.) dried chilli flakes
- 5ml (1 tsp.) olive oil
- Sea salt and freshly ground black pepper, to your liking

INSTRUCTIONS

1. Toss broccoli florets with the remaining ingredients.
2. Roast broccoli florets at 200°C/395°F for 6 to 7 minutes, shaking the basket halfway through the cooking time.

SPICY POTATOES WITH BACON ⑭

Why heat up the whole oven just for roasting a couple of potatoes when you can use your air fryer? Serve these potatoes with a creamy tomato soup and enjoy!

Servings: 4

TOTAL CALORIES: 337
Fat: 5.4g; Carbs: 64.5g; Protein: 9.1g; Sugars: 3.1g; Fibre: 8.1g

INGREDIENTS

- 4 medium potatoes, peeled and diced
- 2g (1/2 tsp.) dried chilli flakes
- Sea salt and freshly ground black pepper, to your liking
- 2 rashers bacon, cut into 2cm-wide lengths

INSTRUCTIONS

1. Sprinkle potatoes with chilli flakes, salt, and black pepper.
2. Bake potatoes at 200°C/395°F for approximately 7 minutes.
3. Top your potatoes with bacon and continue baking for 7 minutes longer, until the bacon is crisp and your potatoes are thoroughly cooked.

7 | *VEGETARIAN AND VEGAN*

DON'T FORGET TO GET THE
TOP RECIPES FROM THIS BOOK
AS

A FREE DOWNLOADABLE PDF IN COLOUR

SCAN THE QR CODE BELOW

Just follow the steps below to access it via the QR Code (the picture code at the bottom of this page) or click the link if you are reading this on your Phone / Device.

1. Unlock your phone & open up the phone's camera
2. Make sure you are using the "back" camera (as if you were taking a photo of someone) and point it towards the QR code at the bottom of the page.
3. Tap your phone's screen exactly where the QR code is.
4. A link / pop up will appear. Simply tap that (and make sure you have internet connection) and the FREE PDF containing all of the colored images should appear.

SCAN ME

① THE BEST CAULIFLOWER CROQUETTES EVER

(IN MINUTES)
PREP 10
COOK 12

Get ready for your dreamy vegetarian meal! With only 162 calories per serving, these cauliflower croquettes are light, delicious, and satisfying. Plus, they are a cinch to make in the air fryer.

Servings: 4

TOTAL CALORIES: 162
Fat: 5.1g; Carbs: 24.4g; Protein: 6.1g; Sugars: 4.6g; Fibre: 3.8g

INGREDIENTS

- 450g (1 lb.) cauliflower, grated
- 1 small carrot, grated
- 1 medium onion, finely chopped
- 2 garlic cloves, finely chopped
- 70g (1/2 cup) all-purpose flour
- Kosher salt and ground black pepper, to taste
- 30g (2 tbsp.) fresh parsley leaves, finely chopped
- 1 medium egg, whisked
- 5ml (1 tsp.) olive oil

INSTRUCTIONS

1. In a mixing bowl, thoroughly combine all the ingredients; mix until everything is well incorporated.
2. Shape the mixture into small balls and transfer them to the lightly oiled air fryer cooking basket; slightly flatten them with a fork.
3. Air fry cauliflower croquettes in the preheated air fryer at 190°C/375°F for 6 minutes.
4. Turn them over and cook for a further 6 minutes.

② BELL PEPPER AND TOFU SALAD

(IN MINUTES)
PREP 10
COOK 15

This old-fashioned salad from a grandma's cookbook goes perfectly with baked beans or roasted potatoes. Other good add-ins include chilli peppers, dill weed, red onions, and so forth.

Servings: 3

TOTAL CALORIES: 265
Fat: 14.8g; Carbs: 18.8g; Protein: 20.1g; Sugars: 0.8g; Fibre: 4.6g

INGREDIENTS

- 3 bell peppers, deveined, deseeded, and halved
- 340g (12 oz.) firm tofu, cubed
- 2 garlic cloves, crushed
- 15ml (1 tbsp.) red wine vinegar
- Sea salt and ground black pepper, to taste
- 15ml (1 tbsp.) olive oil
- 30g (2 tbsp.) fresh parsley leaves, finely chopped

INSTRUCTIONS

1. Arrange the peppers and tofu cubes in a lightly oiled air fryer cooking basket.
2. Roast the peppers and tofu in the preheated air fryer at 200°C/395°F for 15 minutes, shaking the basket once or twice during the cooking time.
3. Slice the peppers into bite-sized strips using a sharp knife.
4. To serve: stir the peppers with the garlic, vinegar, salt, black pepper, and olive oil. Top your salad with the tofu. Garnish your salad with parsley leaves and serve well-chilled or at room temperature.

③ PORTOBELLO MINI PIZZAS

This recipe calls for whole-milk mozzarella, but feel free to use any type of pizza cheese you like! Mozzarella offers the perfect balance of fat content and elasticity for pizza, but good alternatives include Romano, Asiago, or fontina cheese. You can come up with your favourite cheese blend as well.

Servings: 4

TOTAL CALORIES: 265
Fat: 14.8g; Carbs: 18.8g; Protein: 20.1g;
Sugars: 0.8g; Fibre: 4.6g

INGREDIENTS

- 4 portobello mushroom caps, stems removed, washed
- 5ml (1 tsp.) olive oil
- Sea salt and ground black pepper, to taste
- 120ml (1/2 cup) pizza sauce
- 15g (1 tbsp.) Italian seasoning mix
- 1 small bell pepper, seeded and chopped
- 120g (4 oz.) mozzarella cheese, shredded

INSTRUCTIONS

1. Pat dry mushroom caps using tea towels. Toss them with olive oil, salt, and pepper.
2. Make pizza filling: thoroughly combine pizza sauce with the other ingredients. Divide the filling mixture between mushroom caps.
3. Arrange your mushrooms in the lightly oiled air fryer cooking basket. Bake mini pizzas in the preheated air fryer at 190°C/370°F for approximately 10 minutes, until mozzarella has melted.

④ VEGETARIAN CRUSTLESS QUICHE

Who needs any type of flour and pasta when you've got fresh eggs and an air fryer? You can add fresh herbs, olives, or roasted peppers to this amazing vegetarian dish!

Servings: 4

TOTAL CALORIES: 212
Fat: 14.7g; Carbs: 6.4g; Protein: 13.6g;
Sugars: 2.9g; Fibre: 0.8g

INGREDIENTS

- 7 large eggs, beaten
- 60g (4 tbsp.) cream cheese
- 200g (3/4 cup) brown mushrooms, chopped
- 1 small onion, chopped
- 1 bell pepper, seeded and chopped
- 4g (1 tsp.) ground cumin
- 2g (1/2 tsp.) smoked paprika
- Sea salt and ground black pepper, to taste
- 5ml (1 tsp.) olive oil

INSTRUCTIONS

1. Start by preheating your air fryer to 180°C/350°F. Then, brush a baking tray with nonstick cooking oil.
2. In a mixing bowl, thoroughly combine all the ingredients; stir until everything is well mixed.
3. Spoon the mixture into the prepared baking tray.
4. Bake your quiche for approximately 15 minutes, or until set.

LEFTOVER MUFFINS WITH CURRANTS

If you ended up with 1 to 2 cups of leftover porridge, you could make these amazing muffins that everyone will love! The recipe calls for dried currants, but feel free to add your favourite dried fruits, nuts, seeds, and other mix-ins. The recipe is endlessly customizable.

Servings: 4

TOTAL CALORIES: 92
Fat: 3.8g; Carbs: 14.1g; Protein: 1.2g; Sugars: 7.8g; Fibre: 2g

INGREDIENTS

- 120g (1½ cups) porridge
- 75g (1/3 cup) pumpkin puree
- 30ml (2 tbsp.) agave syrup
- 15ml (1 tbsp.) coconut oil, room temperature
- 4g (1 tsp.) pumpkin spice mix
- 60g (1/3 cup) dried currants, chopped

INSTRUCTIONS

1. In a mixing bowl, thoroughly combine the porridge, pumpkin puree, agave syrup, coconut oil, and pumpkin spice mix.
2. Fold in dried currants and give them a gentle stir with a silicone spatula. Scrape the batter into lightly greased cupcakes cases.
3. Bake your muffins in the preheated air fryer at 200°C/395°F for about 10 minutes.

AUBERGINE PARMI-GIANA BAKE

Perfect for a midweek meal, this nutritional vegetarian dish is healthy, delicious, and easy to prepare. When it comes to baking tins, you can use any ovenproof dish in your air fryer.

Servings: 4

TOTAL CALORIES: 136
Fat: 7.8g; Carbs: 11.8g; Protein: 6.1g; Sugars: 5.6g; Fibre: 4.2g

INGREDIENTS

- 450g (1 lb.) aubergine, sliced
- 15ml (1 tbsp.) olive oil
- 2g (1/2 tsp.) onion powder
- 2g (1/2 tsp.) garlic granules
- 1g (1/4 tsp.) cayenne pepper
- Sea salt and ground black pepper, to taste
- 120ml (1/2 cup) pizza sauce
- 60g (2 oz.) Parmesan, grated

INSTRUCTIONS

1. Toss the aubergine with olive oil and spices.
2. Arrange aubergine slices in a lightly greased baking tray; spoon pizza sauce into the baking tray. Lower the tray into the air fryer cooking basket.
3. Bake your aubergine in the preheated air fryer at 190°C/370°F for about 15 minutes.
4. Top your aubergine with Parmesan cheese and continue to bake for 5 minutes more, until the cheese has melted.

THE COMPLETE UK AIR FRYER COOKBOOK

SICHUAN-STYLE GREEN BEANS

(IN MINUTES)
PREP **5**
COOK **7**

The humble green beans get an Asian makeover in this delicious air fryer vegan recipe. You can also add freshly grated vegan Parmesan cheese.

Servings: 3

TOTAL CALORIES: 96

Fat: 2.2g; Carbs: 14.8g; Protein: 6.4g; Sugars: 5.6g; Fibre: 5.2g

INGREDIENTS

- 450g (1 lb.) green beans, trimmed
- 5ml (1 tsp.) sesame oil
- 2g (1/2 tsp.) garlic granules
- 2g (1/2 tsp.) Sichuan pepper
- 1g (1/4 tsp.) cayenne pepper
- 1 small knob of ginger, peeled and minced
- 15ml (1 tbsp.) dark soy sauce
- 30g (2 tbsp.) nutritional yeast flakes
- 30g (2 tbsp.) roasted cashews, finely chopped
- 2 spring onions, sliced

INSTRUCTIONS

1. Toss green beans with sesame oil, spices, ginger, and soy sauce.
2. Air fry green beans in the preheated air fryer at 200°C/395°F for 7 minutes more, until crisp-tender.
3. In the meantime, mix nutritional yeast flakes and roasted cashews to make the vegan "Parmesan."
4. Garnish green beans with the vegan "Parmesan" and spring onions, then serve immediately.

JACKET POTATOES WITH CHEESE & CHIVES

(IN MINUTES)
PREP **5**
COOK **40**

To prepare whole potatoes, poke them with a fork or sharp knife, just enough to pierce the skin; This will prevent the baked potato from bursting in the air fryer. Serve baked potatoes with the slaw on the side.

Servings: 2

TOTAL CALORIES: 473

Fat: 14.5g; Carbs: 78g; Protein: 10.6g; Sugars: 3.6g; Fibre: 5.6g

INGREDIENTS

- 4 medium russet potatoes, unpeeled
- 60ml (4 tbsp.) cream cheese, room temperature
- 8g (2 tsp.) butter
- 15g (1 tbsp.) chives
- Sea salt and ground black pepper, to taste

INSTRUCTIONS

1. Prick holes in the unpeeled potatoes using a fork or sharp knife. Place russet potatoes in the lightly greased air fryer cooking basket.
2. Bake your potatoes at 190°C/380°F for about 40 minutes.
3. Split your potatoes and add your toppings. Add salt and pepper and serve immediately.

POTATO AND PARSNIP FRITTERS

(IN MINUTES)
PREP 5
COOK 15

Make these delicious fritters with simple ingredients you already have in your kitchen. Serve warm fritters with a mayo sauce on the side.

Servings: 3

TOTAL CALORIES: 453
Fat: 5.5g; Carbs: 91g; Protein: 11.3g;
Sugars: 6.4g; Fibre: 8.3g

iNGREDiENTS

• 3 medium russet potatoes, peeled and grated
• 1 large parsnip, grated
• 1 small onion, finely chopped
• 1 garlic clove, minced
• 15g (1 tbsp.) fresh parsley, chopped
• 15g (1 tbsp.) milled flaxseed
• 40g (1/3 cup) crushed crackers
• 120g (1 cup) all-purpose flour
• Sea salt and ground black pepper, to taste
• 5ml (1 tsp.) olive oil

iNSTRUCTiONS

1. In a mixing bowl, thoroughly combine all ingredients. Shape the mixture into small patties and place them in the lightly greased cooking basket.
2. Bake your fritters at 180°C/360°F for 15 minutes, until thoroughly cooked and crispy on the outside.

VEGAN BUTTERNUT SQUASH BURGERS

(IN MINUTES)
PREP 10
COOK 22

Here are the perfect budget-friendly, plant-based burgers for the whole family! Other good topping ideas include tofu mayonnaise, stone-ground mustard, fresh tomatoes, cornichons, and iceberg lettuce. Enjoy!

Servings: 4

TOTAL CALORIES: 222
Fat: 3.3g; Carbs: 44.7g; Protein: 6.6g;
Sugars: 9.5g; Fibre: 4.6g

iNGREDiENTS

• 550g (4 heaping cups) butternut squash, peeled and sliced into roughly 1-cm discs
• 5ml (1 tsp.) chilli oil (or regular olive oil)
• Sea salt and ground black pepper, to taste
• 2g (1/2 tsp.) dried dill (optional)
• 4 burger buns
• 1 small leek, chopped
• 2 handfuls rocket lettuce
• 5ml (1 tsp.) mustard
• 30ml (2 tbsp.) tomato ketchup

iNSTRUCTiONS

1. Toss butternut squash with chilli oil, salt, pepper, and dill (if using). Then, transfer the butternut squash discs to the lightly greased air fryer cooking basket.
2. Roast butternut squash at 170°C/340°F for about 22 minutes, until fork tender.
3. Assemble your burgers with burger buns, roasted butternut squash, leek, lettuce, mustard, and ketchup.

GRILLED TOFU SANDWICH

(IN MINUTES)
PREP
5
COOK
7

Did you know that you can make a perfect grilled tofu sandwich in your air fryer? How to press your tofu? Place the folded paper towels on a cutting board; then, lower your tofu onto the paper towels. Place another layer of paper towels (or a tea towel) on top. Afterwards, place a bowl or heavy frying-pan on top, and let it sit for at least 30 minutes.

Servings: 2

TOTAL CALORIES: 242
Fat: 6.3g; Carbs: 33.7g; Protein: 13.6g;
Sugars: 3.9g; Fibre: 5g

INGREDIENTS

- 4 thin slices bread
- 4 thin slices firm tofu, pressed
- 30g (2 tbsp.) hummus
- 2 slices tomatoes
- 1/2 small red onion, thinly sliced
- 30g (2 tbsp.) coleslaw

INSTRUCTIONS

1. Assemble two sandwiches with bread, tofu, and hummus.
2. Toast your sandwiches at 200°C/400° F for about 7 minutes.
3. Garnish your sandwiches with tomatoes, red onion, and coleslaw.

RED BEETROOT FALAFEL

(IN MINUTES)
PREP
5
COOK
20

Jazz up your favourite vegetarian wrap by adding fresh beetroots! Serve warm falafel in Middle Eastern-style flatbread or classic tortilla. Popular fixings include tahini sauce, mustard, mayo, yoghurt sauce, and so forth.

Servings: 4

TOTAL CALORIES: 265
Fat: 6.6g; Carbs: 40.7g; Protein: 11.8g;
Sugars: 7.9g; Fibre: 7.5g

INGREDIENTS

- 250g (1 cup) dried chickpeas, soaked overnight
- 1 medium red beetroot, peeled and grated
- 60g (4 tbsp.) breadcrumbs
- 2g (1/2 tsp.) baking soda
- 1 large garlic clove
- 2 parsley sprigs
- 1 small onion, peeled and diced
- 1g (1/4 tsp.) ground cumin
- Sea salt and freshly ground black pepper, to taste
- 15ml (1 tbsp.) olive oil

INSTRUCTIONS

1. Add all ingredients to a bowl of your blender or food processor. Blend until everything is well combined.
2. Shape the mixture into equal balls using damp hands; arrange them in the lightly greased cooking basket.
3. Air fry your falafel at 190°C/380°F for about 20 minutes, shaking the basket halfway through the cooking time.

BBQ TEMPEH WITH BRUSSELS SPROUTS

Enjoy a healthy, plant-based meal that can keep you full and happy for longer! Tempeh can significantly reduce cholesterol levels and blood sugar; it can also protect your body from inflammation and keep your bones healthy and strong!

Servings: 4

TOTAL CALORIES: 178
Fat: 10.2g; Carbs: 12.7g; Protein: 12.5g; Sugars: 2.5g; Fibre: 2.5g

INGREDIENTS

- 220g (8 oz.) tempeh, pressed and cubed
- 225g (1/2 lb.) Brussels sprouts, halved
- 2g (1/2 tsp.) garlic granules
- 4g (1 tsp.) dried parsley flakes
- 15ml (1 tbsp.) olive oil
- 15ml (1 tbsp.) soy sauce
- 15ml (1 tbsp.) tomato sauce
- 4g (1 tsp.) smoked paprika
- Sea salt and freshly ground black pepper, to taste

INSTRUCTIONS

1. Toss the tempeh and Brussels sprouts with the remaining ingredients.
2. Now, arrange the tempeh and Brussels sprouts in the lightly greased cooking basket.
3. Air fry the tempeh and Brussels sprouts at 190°C/390°F for 10 minutes; shake the cooking basket and continue to cook for a further 5 minutes.

QUINOA BURGERS

Quinoa burgers are a staple of a vegan diet. You can experiment and add your favourite aromatics for a fresh twist on your healthy, plant-based burgers! You can use mint, thyme, ground cumin, or ground bay leaf.

Servings: 4

TOTAL CALORIES: 169
Fat: 3.6g; Carbs: 30g; Protein: 5.3g; Sugars: 2.2g; Fibre: 4.4g

INGREDIENTS

- 200g (1½ cups) quinoa, cooked and rinsed
- 1 small onion, finely chopped
- 2 garlic cloves, crushed
- 15g (1 tbsp.) grill seasoning
- 15g (1 tbsp.) milled flaxseed
- 100g (1 cup) cooked potatoes
- 50g (1/4 cup) all-purpose flour
- Sea salt and ground black pepper, to taste
- 4ml (1 tsp.) olive oil

INSTRUCTIONS

1. In a mixing bowl, thoroughly combine all ingredients. Shape the mixture into patties and arrange them in the lightly greased air fryer cooking basket.
2. Cook quinoa burgers at 180°C/360°F for approximately 17 minutes, until thoroughly cooked and crispy on the outside.

GARBANZO BEAN STUFFED SWEET POTATOES

Prepare a healthy and light vegetarian dish with this rustic, herb stuffing to delight your beloved one! For a vegan version, substitute butter with tahini.

Servings: 2

TOTAL CALORIES: 273
Fat: 6.2g; Carbs: 47.7g; Protein: 8.2g;
Sugars: 10.1g; Fibre: 9g

INGREDIENTS

- 2 medium sweet potatoes, unpeeled
- 8g (2 tsp). butter
- 1 small onion, chopped
- 15g (1 tbsp.) fresh cilantro, roughly chopped
- 15g (1 tbsp.) fresh parsley, roughly chopped
- 160g (1 cup) canned garbanzo beans, drained and rinsed
- Sea salt and ground black pepper, to taste

INSTRUCTIONS

1. Prick holes in the unpeeled potatoes using a fork. Place sweet potatoes in the lightly greased air fryer cooking basket.
2. Bake sweet potatoes at 180°C/360°F for about 35 minutes.
3. Split your potatoes and top them with butter, onion, cilantro, parsley, and garbanzo beans. Add sea salt and pepper, then serve immediately.

8 | DESSERTS

DON'T FORGET TO GET THE
TOP RECIPES FROM THIS BOOK
AS
A FREE DOWNLOADABLE PDF IN COLOUR

SCAN THE QR CODE BELOW

Just follow the steps below to access it via the QR Code (the picture code at the bottom of this page) or click the link if you are reading this on your Phone / Device.

1. Unlock your phone & open up the phone's camera
2. Make sure you are using the "back" camera (as if you were taking a photo of someone) and point it towards the QR code at the bottom of the page.
3. Tap your phone's screen exactly where the QR code is.
4. A link / pop up will appear. Simply tap that (and make sure you have internet connection) and the FREE PDF containing all of the colored images should appear.

AUTUMN PEAR CRUMBLE

Here's the recipe for a family favourite autumn dessert! Dark brown soft sugar is the perfect sweetener for this crumble, but feel free to use any type of brown sugar or golden caster sugar.

Servings: 4

TOTAL CALORIES: 533

Protein: 58.77g | Fats: 57.34g | Carbs: 62.85g

INGREDIENTS

- 2 medium pears, peeled, cored, and sliced
- 15g (1 tbsp.) arrowroot powder
- 30g (2 tbsp.) brown sugar

Topping:

- 40g (1/2 cup) old-fashioned rolled oats
- 40g (1/3 cup) all-purpose flour
- 50g (1/4 cup) brown sugar
- 15g (1 tbsp.) peanut butter
- 100g (1/2 cup) coconut oil, melted
- 1g (1/4 tsp.) ground cinnamon
- 1g (1/4 tsp.) grated nutmeg
- 70g (1/2 cup) almonds, chopped

INSTRUCTIONS

1. Toss your pears with arrowroot powder and sugar. Arrange the pears in a lightly greased baking tray.
2. In a mixing dish, thoroughly combine all topping ingredients. Sprinkle topping ingredients over the pear layer. Place the baking tray in the air fryer cooking basket.
3. Bake the pear crumble in the preheated air fryer at 165°C/330°F for about 35 minutes. Let it cool for 10 minutes before serving.

FRIED PINEAPPLE RINGS

Don't miss this healthy-ish dessert recipe for fried pineapple rings! It is easy to prepare and fun to eat! Serve with ice cream and enjoy!

Servings: 2

TOTAL CALORIES: 231

Fat: 7.2g; Carbs: 45.4g; Protein: 1.7g; Sugars: 34.3g; Fibre: 4.6g

INGREDIENTS

- 4 rings of pineapple, fresh or canned (approximately ¼-inch thick)
- 15g (1 tbsp.) coconut oil, melted
- 1g (1/4 tsp.) cinnamon powder
- 1ml (1/4 tsp.) pure vanilla extract

INSTRUCTIONS

1. Toss the pineapple rings with the other ingredients. Arrange the pineapple rings in a lightly greased baking tray.
2. Roast the pineapple rings in the preheated air fryer at 165°C/330°F for about 30 minutes.

3 CHOCOLATE CUPCAKES

If you like chocolate and cupcakes, you will love this recipe! These cupcakes are endlessly customizable, so you can use your favourite mix-ins such as nuts, dried fruits, and spices.

Servings: 4

TOTAL CALORIES: 351

Fat: 17.2g; Carbs: 50.4g; Protein: 6.2g; Sugars: 27.3g; Fibre: 4.6g

INGREDIENTS

- 1 large egg, beaten
- 2ml (1/2 tsp.) vanilla essence
- 2ml (1/3 tsp). cinnamon powder
- A pinch of salt
- 60g (1/2 cup) butter, softened
- 100g (1/2 cup) brown sugar
- 70g (1/2 cup) all-purpose flour
- 2g (1/2) tsp. baking powder
- 50g (1/2 cup) cocoa powder
- 30g (2 tbsp.) dark chocolate chips
- Buttercream, to decorate (optional)

INSTRUCTIONS

1. Begin by preheating your air fryer to 175°C/350°F. Now, brush the sides and bottom of cupcake cases with nonstick cooking spray.
2. Beat the egg with spices until pale and frothy. Next, gradually stir in the butter, sugar, flour, baking powder, and cocoa powder. Stir to combine well.
3. Afterwards, fold in the chocolate chips and gently stir to combine. Spoon the batter into the cupcake cases; press them with the back of a spoon.
4. Bake your cupcakes for approximately 20 minutes, until a tester comes out dry and clean. Leave your cupcakes to cool completely before adding buttercream, if using.

ALMOND FIG BARS

Make granola-style almond bars in your air fryer in no time! This is a good alternative to expensive and not-so-healthy, store-bought energy bars. Devour!

Servings: 6

TOTAL CALORIES: 291

Fat: 17g; Carbs: 31.1g; Protein: 7.3g; Sugars: 16.3g; Fibre: 4.1g

INGREDIENTS

- 50g (3.5 tbsp.) butter
- 50g (6.7 tbsp.) pepitas, chopped
- 100g (1 cup) oats
- 25g (3 tbsp.) sesame seeds
- 25g (3 tbsp.) almonds, chopped
- 30ml (2 tbsp.) honey
- 50g (1/4 cup) light muscovado sugar
- 2g (1/2 tsp.) ground cinnamon
- 4 dried figs, chopped

INSTRUCTIONS

1. Begin by preheating your air fryer to 180°C/360°F.
2. In a mixing bowl, thoroughly combine all the ingredients. Spoon the batter into a parchment-lined baking tray; press down lightly using a silicone spatula.
3. Bake it for approximately 20 minutes. Let it cool and cut it into bars.

GRILLED FRUIT SKEWERS

This is the perfect dessert to accompany a busy week-night dinner. Easy, healthy, and delicious, this is a great way to get kids to eat more fruits.

Servings: 4

TOTAL CALORIES: 351
Fat: 17.2g; Carbs: 50.4g; Protein: 6.2g; Sugars: 27.3g; Fibre: 4.6g

INGREDIENTS

- 1 mango, diced into bite-sized chunks
- 12 grape seeds
- 8 fresh apricots, pitted and halved
- 15ml (1 tbsp.) honey
- 5ml (1 tsp.) fresh lemon juice
- 3ml (1/2 tsp.) pure vanilla extract

INSTRUCTIONS

1. Begin by preheating your air fryer to 180°C/360°F.
2. Toss fruits with honey, lemon juice, and vanilla; now tread fruit pieces on soaked bamboo skewers.
3. Air fry fruit skewers for approximately 10 minutes.

GOLDEN SYRUP PANCAKE CUPS

Here is a great recipe for Shrove Tuesday! If you like traditional British pancakes, these pancake cups will blow your mind away. You can serve them with golden syrup, maple syrup, fresh or frozen berries, jam, and so forth.

Servings: 4

TOTAL CALORIES: 221
Fat: 2.7g; Carbs: 40.4g; Protein: 6.6g; Sugars: 2.3g; Fibre: 1.6g

INGREDIENTS
- 1 large egg, beaten
- 60ml (1/2 cup) almond milk
- 3ml (1/2 tsp.) vanilla
- 200g (7 oz.) all-purpose flour
- A pinch of kosher salt
- A pinch of ground cinnamon
- 5g (1 tsp.) butter, melted

INSTRUCTIONS

1. Beat the egg with almond milk and vanilla until pale and frothy. Gradually stir in the other ingredients; beat with an electric mixer to ensure no lumps are created.
2. Spoon the batter into the cupcake cases.
3. Bake pancake cups at 180°C/360°F for about 15 minutes, until golden brown on the top.

TRADITIONAL FLAPJACKS

(IN MINUTES)
PREP **10**
COOK **20**

When you are bored of having oatmeal for breakfast, you can hide it in your dessert! This is a good way to use up the porridge oats, butter, and golden syrup.

Servings: 4

TOTAL CALORIES: 319

Fat: 14.4g; Carbs: 44g; Protein: 5.5g; Sugars: 23g; Fibre: 3.6g

INGREDIENTS

- 125g (1½ cups) porridge oats
- 30g (2 tbsp.) granola
- 60g (4¼ tbsp.) butter
- A pinch of sea salt
- 2g (1/4 tsp.) cinnamon powder
- 2g (1/4 tsp.) turmeric powder
- 60g (1/2 cup) brown sugar
- 30ml (2 tbsp.) golden syrup

INSTRUCTIONS

1. Begin by preheating your air fryer to 175°C/350°F. Now, brush the sides and bottom of a baking tray with nonstick cooking spray.
2. In your blender or food processor, thoroughly combine all the ingredients until everything is well mixed. Spoon the batter into the baking tray; press them with the back of a spoon.
3. Bake your flapjacks for approximately 20 minutes, until a tester comes out dry and clean.
4. Leave your flapjacks to cool for 10 minutes before slicing and serving.

ARMAGNAC PRUNE MINI TARTS

(IN MINUTES)
PREP **10**
COOK **35**

This is the secret to the best mini tarts ever – boozy prunes! Make sure to soak your prunes in Armanac before cooking. This is a real choccy, fruity heaven!

Servings: 5

TOTAL CALORIES: 502

Fat: 34.4g; Carbs: 40.4g; Protein: 8.2g; Sugars: 16.3g; Fibre: 3.6g

INGREDIENTS

- 3 medium eggs, separated
- 50g (1/4 cup) granulated sugar
- 125g (3/4 cup) dark chocolate chunks, melted (70-85% cacao solids)
- 1g (1/4 tsp.) ground cloves
- 2g (1/2 tsp.) ground cinnamon
- 4g (1 tsp.) orange zest
- 60g (1/2 cup) pitted prunes, (soaked in 25ml of Armagnac) and then pureed
- 100g (1/4 cup + 3 tbsp.) butter
- 45g (1/3 cup) plain flour
- 45g (1/3 cup) ground walnuts

INSTRUCTIONS

1. Start by preheating your air fryer to 180°C/360°F. Brush the air fryer tartlet moulds with a small amount of butter.
2. Beat egg whites with 1 tablespoon of the sugar until the mixture forms hard peaks. In another bowl, whip the egg yolks with the remaining ingredients. Fold in the melted chocolate and the remaining wet ingredients; mix to combine.
3. In a separate bowl, thoroughly combine the dry ingredients. Slowly stir in the egg whites, making sure you don't lose their airy texture. Carefully fold in the chocolate mixture and gently stir to combine well.
4. Spoon the batter into tartlet moulds and cook for about 35 minutes, until a toothpick inserted in the centre of your tarts comes out dry and clean.

CHOCOLATE CHIP COOKIES

(IN MINUTES)
PREP 10
COOK 20

If you are not in a hurry, you can place the dough in the fridge for 2 to 3 hours; flavours will deepen over time. You can add raisins, dried currants, and chopped nuts to a chilled cookie dough.

Servings: 8

TOTAL CALORIES: 273
Fat: 13.3g; Carbs: 34g; Protein: 4.5g; Sugars: 11.8g; Fibre: 1.6g

INGREDIENTS

- 200g (7 oz.) all-purpose flour
- 4g (1 tsp.) baking powder
- 110ml (4 oz.) agave syrup
- 60g (1/2 cup) butter, room temperature
- 3ml (1/2 tsp.) vanilla extract
- 1g (1/4 tsp.) ground cloves
- A pinch of cinnamon powder
- 1 large egg, beaten, room temperature
- 60ml (4 tbsp.) plain almond milk
- 60ml (2 oz) double cream
- 60g (2 oz) chocolate chips

INSTRUCTIONS

1. Begin by preheating your air fryer to 175°C/350°F.
2. In a mixing bowl, thoroughly combine the dry ingredients; mix until your mixture resembles breadcrumbs. In another bowl, mix all the liquid ingredients. Add the wet mixture to the dry ingredients; fold in chocolate chips and stir to combine well.
3. Now form balls of cookie dough using an ice cream scoop and place them on the parchment-lined baking tin.
4. Bake your cookies in the preheated air fryer for 15 minutes. Let them sit on a cooling rack for about 10 minutes before serving.

CLASSIC MINCE PIES

(IN MINUTES)
PREP 10
COOK 20

If you do not want to use brandy, you can opt for sherry or orange juice for mince pies. An air fryer is the perfect tool to make mince pies – they are nice and golden brown around the edges, and soft in the middle.

Servings: 8

TOTAL CALORIES: 503
Fat: 27.2g; Carbs: 62.2g; Protein: 3.5g; Sugars: 35.3g; Fibre: 11.6g

INGREDIENTS

Filling:
- 300g quality mincemeat
- 1 splash of brandy
- 1 apple, chopped
- A pinch of cinnamon powder
- A pinch of ginger powder
- 4g (1 tsp.) lemon zest

Pastry:
- 185g (1½ cups) all-purpose flour
- 260g (4.5 oz.) butter, unsalted and softened
- 125g (1/2 cup) caster sugar, plus extra for sprinkling
- 1 medium egg

INSTRUCTIONS

1. Mix the mincemeat, brandy, apple chunks, cinnamon, ginger, and lemon zest
2. Place the flour and butter in a mixing bowl; rub together to a crumb consistency. Stir in the sugar and egg and mix to combine well.
3. Roll out your dough to the same thickness; cut out 16 circles using a tumbler. Divide the mincemeat filling between 8 circles; place the lids on the top and crimp the edges together.
4. Now, brush the sides and bottom of a baking tin with nonstick cooking spray.
5. Bake mince pies at 180°C/360°F for about 20 minutes, working with batches, if needed.

OLD-FASHIONED CINNAMON APPLES

(IN MINUTES)
PREP **5**
COOK **10**

Perfectly cooked and absolutely delicious, this simple dessert is made with just a few ingredients! Apples pair amazingly with aromatics such as cinnamon powder and sweeteners such as agave syrup.
Servings: 3

TOTAL CALORIES: 131
Fat: 4.9g; Carbs: 24.4g; Protein: 0.4g;
Sugars: 18.3g; Fibre: 3.6g

INGREDIENTS

- 3 small apples, cored and cut into wedges
- 15g (1 tbsp.) coconut oil, melted
- 1g (1/4 tsp.) cinnamon powder
- 10ml (2 tsp.) agave syrup
- 1ml (1/4 tsp.) pure vanilla extract

INSTRUCTIONS

1. Toss the apple wedges with the other ingredients. Arrange the apple wedges in a lightly greased baking tray.
2. Roast the apple wedges in the preheated air fryer at 180°C/360°F for about 10 minutes.

DAD'S BREAD PUDDING

(IN MINUTES)
PREP **5**
COOK **20**

Here's the recipe for the best holiday pudding ever! Serve warm pudding with whipped vanilla-spiked cream, or chocolate ice cream. Dig in!

Servings: 4

TOTAL CALORIES: 230
Fat: 8.7g; Carbs: 31.4g; Protein: 6.7g;
Sugars: 17.6g; Fibre: 1.6g

INGREDIENTS

- 6 thin bread slices, cubed
- 1 small egg, beaten
- 5ml (1 tsp.) whiskey
- 60g (4 tbsp.) brown sugar
- 250ml (1 cup) almond milk
- 3ml (1/2 tsp.) vanilla extract
- A pinch of ground cloves
- A pinch of ground cinnamon
- A pinch of kosher salt
- 30g (2 tbsp.) pecans, chopped

INSTRUCTIONS

1. In a mixing bowl, thoroughly combine all the ingredients; stir well using a spatula and set it aside for about 30 minutes to soak.
2. Spoon the pudding mixture into a deep baking tin.
3. Bake your bread pudding at 180°C/360°F for about 20 minutes.

EVERYTHING COOKIES WITH CHERRIES

This recipe is endlessly customizable – you can add dried apricots, prunes, or chopped pecans to cookie dough. If you want crisper cookies, set the timer for a couple more minutes.

Servings: 8

TOTAL CALORIES: 213
Fat: 8.3g; Carbs: 31.4g; Protein: 3.5g; Sugars: 18g; Fibre: 0.7g

INGREDIENTS

- 100g (3.5 oz.) all-purpose flour
- 100g (3.5 oz.) quick-cooking oats
- 4g (1 tsp.) baking powder
- 110g (4 oz.) brown sugar
- 2ml (1/4 tsp.) vanilla extract
- A pinch of coarse salt
- 2 small eggs, beaten, room temperature
- 60g (1/2 cup) butter, room temperature
- 60g (1/2 cup) toffees, roughly chopped
- 60g (1/2 cup) dried cherries, pitted

INSTRUCTIONS

1. Begin by preheating your air fryer to 175°C/350°F.
2. In a mixing bowl, thoroughly combine the dry ingredients; mix until your mixture resembles breadcrumbs. In another bowl, mix all the liquid ingredients. Add the wet mixture to the dry ingredients; fold in toffees and dried cherries.
3. Now form balls of cookie dough using an ice cream scoop and place them on the parchment-lined baking tin. Work in batches, if needed.
4. Bake your cookies in the preheated air fryer for 15 minutes. Leave the cookies on wire racks to firm up.

CINNAMON BANANA MUFFINS

If you love banana bread, you will love these muffins! Perfect for busy mornings and family gatherings, you can serve them for breakfast or dessert. They will disappear in minutes!

Servings: 4

TOTAL CALORIES: 259
Fat: 9.6g; Carbs: 47.3g; Protein: 4.7g; Sugars: 21.3g; Fibre: 5.6g

INGREDIENTS

- 1 large banana, mashed
- 4g (1 tsp.) cinnamon powder
- A pinch of salt
- 30g (1/4 cup) coconut oil, room temperature
- 50g (1/4 cup) golden caster sugar
- 70g (1/2 cup) all-purpose flour
- 4g (1 tsp.) baking powder
- 50g (1/2 cup) cocoa powder
- 30g (2 tbsp.) raisins
- Buttercream, to decorate (optional)

INSTRUCTIONS

1. Begin by preheating your air fryer to 175°C/350°F.
2. In a mixing bowl, thoroughly combine all the dry ingredients. In a separate bowl, mix the liquid ingredients. After that, add the liquid mixture to the dry ingredients; mix to combine.
3. Afterwards, fold in the raisins and gently stir to combine. Spoon the batter into the lightly greased cupcake cases.
4. Bake your muffins in the preheated air fryer for approximately 20 minutes. Leave your cupcakes to cool completely before frosting, if using.

ABOUT THE AUTHOR

We are Fearne Prentice!

A group of Chefs & Recipe Writers decided to team up and work together to create the best UK Cookbooks on the market!

See, by working together we can alleviate each other's weaknesses and create the most delicious recipes for you to enjoy.

Whether it's needing some UK Air Fryer classics to spice up your parties, or some slow cooker favorites to warm your winters we can promise we've got you covered.

We'd also LOVE to hear your feedback and see your pictures when you create our recipes! Please share them with us and leave a review!

Now, enough talking, it's time to get back to cooking!

Don't forget to check out these other books by Fearne Prentice!

Printed in Great Britain
by Amazon

16235718R00045